The Master Musicians Series

MENDELSSOHN

VOLUMES IN THE MASTER MUSICIANS SERIES

Bartók   *Lajos Lesznai*
Beethoven   *Marion M. Scott*
Bellini   *Leslie Orrey*
Berlioz   *J. H. Elliot*
Bizet   *Winton Dean*
Brahms   *Peter Latham*
Bruckner   *Derek Watson*
Chopin   *Arthur Hedley*
Debussy   *Edward Lockspeiser*
Delius   *Alan Jefferson*
Dvořák   *Alec Robertson*
Elgar   *Ian Parrott*
Franck   *Laurence Davies*
Grieg   *John Horton*
Handel   *Percy M. Young*
Haydn   *Rosemary Hughes*
Liszt   *Walter Beckett*

Mahler   *Michael Kennedy*
Mendelssohn   *Philip Radcliffe*
Monteverdi   *Denis Arnold*
Mozart   *Eric Blom*
Mussorgsky   *M. D. Calvocoressi*
Purcell   *Sir Jack Westrup*
Rakhmaninov   *Geoffrey Norris*
Schubert   *Arthur Hutchings*
Schumann   *Joan Chissell*
Sibelius   *Robert Layton*
Smetana   *John Clapham*
Richard Strauss   *Michael Kennedy*
Stravinsky   *Francis Routh*
Tchaikovsky   *Edward Garden*
Vaughan Williams   *James Day*
Verdi   *Dyneley Hussey*
Wagner   *Robert L. Jacobs*

IN PREPARATION

Bach   *Basil Lam*
Berg   *Nicholas Chadwick*
Prokofiev   *Rita McAllister*
Ravel   *Roger Nichols*

Schoenberg   *Malcolm MacDonald*
Shostakovich   *Geoffrey Norris*
Vivaldi   *Michael Talbot*

THE MASTER MUSICIANS SERIES

MENDELSSOHN

by
Philip Radcliffe

M.A., Mus.Bac.(Cantab.)

With eight pages of plates
and music examples in the text

London
J. M. DENT & SONS LTD

Made in Great Britain
at the
Aldine Press · Letchworth · Herts
for
J. M. DENT & SONS LTD
Aldine House · Albemarle Street · London
First published 1954
Last revised 1976
Paperback edition 1976

Hardback ISBN: 0 460 03123 6
Paperback ISBN: 0 460 02180 x

TO
ARTHUR TREW

PREFACE

FOR this only a few words are needed. From his earliest days Mendelssohn was for ever making social contacts, and it is not surprising that the story of his life has often been told, that many have written reminiscences of his personality, and that his music, though much of it is inadequately known at the moment, is still for the most part accessible. This book can therefore make no claim to be a work of original scholarship or research; it aims rather at presenting a clear view of Mendelssohn's life and works, coloured neither by the exaggerated hero-worship by which they were at first surrounded nor by the equally exaggerated denigration that followed. We can see more easily now the curiously uneven quality of his output, and distinguish between the works that merely reflect the social background against which they were written and those that glow with an individual imagination; similarly his personality can be seen now as something more complex and contradictory than was often imagined. It is hoped that this book may at least fill others with the curiosity to pursue these investigations further.

P. F. R.

1954.

THE author has taken the opportunity of a second edition to correct a few misprints.

PREFACE TO NEW EDITION

THE revised edition of this book contains addenda dealing with works by Mendelssohn that have been published since the book first appeared, and there are minor changes and additions.

P. F. R.

1967.

NOTE TO THE 1976 REPRINT

Since the 1967 edition of this book, a number of early works by Mendelssohn have been published, including the remainder of the String Symphonies. In order to cover these, a few more pages have been added.

P. F. R.

CONTENTS

ILLUSTRATIONS

Between pages 54 and 55

CHAPTER I

1809–1824

IF the life of Mendelssohn is set beside those of most great composers, its most striking feature is its comparative ease and luxuriousness. Inevitably this has affected estimates of him both as a man and as a composer, but not always in the same direction. For many years the fact that he was not one of those wild, difficult bohemians, but a pleasant-mannered, cultured gentleman, undoubtedly endeared him to a very large section of society, especially in England. Handel had been a great public figure, but of a formidably volcanic disposition, with few intimate friends; Mendelssohn they could regard more as one of themselves, and they could find in his music a reflection of his personal charm and geniality. From this attitude of instinctive, uncritical affection there was bound to be a reaction—his charm was thought to be a symptom of superficiality and his cultured and luxurious environment to have led merely to sluggishness and complacence.

In all of this there is a certain amount of dangerous half-truth; the intense emotional struggles of a Beethoven or a Wagner played no part in Mendelssohn's life. But there can be no doubt that he was a person of almost superabundant vitality, and by no means a monster of immaculate correctness. Some excerpts from the letters of Fanny Horsley illustrate this well: 'Felix was very lachrimose and rushed four times in and out of the room in a very phrensied manner. I gazed at him for some time in such deep amaze that I am sure at last he perceived it. What an odd-tempered creature he is.' 'Mamma and Mary think Mendelssohn will never marry. I do, that is if he does not plague his mistress to death before the day arrives.' On one occasion the same young

I

lady complained that 'he was dressed very badly, and looked in sad want of the piece of soap and nail-brush which I have so often threatened to offer him.' Many other contemporary records testify to his exceptionally restless and volatile temperament, with moods that were liable to change from one extreme to another with a kind of childish abandonment and impulsiveness.

When considering Mendelssohn's life it is important to remember that the circumstances in which he grew up were still a quite recent development in the history of his family. It would indeed be hard to imagine a greater contrast than that between Felix's childhood and his grandfather Moses Mendelssohn's, who was born in 1729, at a time when the gulf between Jews and Gentiles in Germany seemed unbridgeable. Sebastian Hensel's *Die Familie Mendelssohn* contains a vivid account of the humiliations that the Jews were compelled to undergo at that time. Typical in its gratuitous insolence was the law passed by Frederick the Great whereby every Jew was compelled to celebrate his marriage by purchasing from the royal china factory in Berlin such goods as would otherwise have been unsaleable; as the result of this Moses Mendelssohn had to buy twenty life-size china apes. He was a man of very great distinction, eminent as a philosopher and as a champion of Jewish emancipation, and he was portrayed by his friend Lessing in the title-part of the play *Nathan der Weise*. But it was only towards the end of his life that he attained to any kind of tranquillity; his early years were a long struggle, sustained by a burning idealism and a finely balanced mind. He was small and humpbacked, largely as the result of overwork and nervous strain; this was inherited to a far lesser extent by his grand-daughter Fanny. He resisted attempts to persuade him to become a Christian, and it is a great tribute to his personality that in the face of so much racial prejudice he was so widely loved and respected.

His wife, Fromet Gugenheim, bore him three sons and three daughters; two of the sons, Joseph and Abraham, Felix's father, became bankers. The eldest daughter, Dorothea, married as her second husband the poet Friedrich von Schlegel and produced some literary works which appeared under his name. But of these three sisters it was the third, Henriette, who played the most prominent part in Felix's life. Known by her nephews and nieces as 'Tante Jette,' she was for some years headmistress of a school in Paris and became governess to the daughter of General Sebastiani. Sebastian Hensel describes the appointment as 'a brilliant misery,' adding: 'What self-sacrifice did Henriette devote to the ungrateful task of making this meagre French soil fruitful by German diligence!' Fanny Sebastiani, an attractive but not particularly intelligent child, eventually married the son of the Duc de Praslin, by whom she was subsequently murdered in 1847. After the marriage, which took place in 1824, Henriette returned to Berlin and was in close touch with her brother Abraham's family until her death in 1831. She was evidently a warm-hearted and sensitive personality, perhaps somewhat anxious and intense; a letter written to her nephew on his twentieth birthday opens memorably: 'My poor Felix; in ten years no longer a boy!'

Abraham Mendelssohn, 'formerly the son of my father, and now the father of my son,' as he later described himself, was born at Berlin in 1776. During the early years of the nineteenth century he was working in a bank in Paris, and it was on the journey back from Paris to Berlin that he met Leah Salomon, who soon became his wife. After the marriage Abraham, though much attracted by Paris, abandoned his post there at the request of his wife, whose mother had disliked the idea of her daughter 'marrying a clerk,' and settled at Hamburg as a partner of his brother Joseph, living in his house with their mother, by this time a widow. Leah was accomplished as a musician and an artist, and a keen student of English, French, Italian and, last but not least, Homer, whom she apparently read in secret, as though ashamed of so unwomanly an excess of erudition. Abraham, if less obviously distinguished than his father and his son, was a remarkable character, full of the deep family affection so characteristic of his race. Though not a practical musician, he had strong musical instincts which his son Felix held in high respect, venturing to disagree with him only on the merits of Beethoven's late works. These Abraham was unable to stomach, and his well-meant advice to Felix to eschew fairyland in favour of what was earnest and grand showed an incomplete understanding of his son's genius. But he was a most devoted if autocratic parent and all his family, Felix in particular, were deeply attached to him. The letters that he wrote to them when they were children illustrate well his patriarchal benevolence:

You, dear Fanny, have written your first letter very nicely; the second, however, was a little hasty. It does you credit that you do not like B's bad jokes; I do not approve of them either, and it is wicked to try to make people laugh at what is beautiful and good.

And later, in the same letter, to Felix:

Your letters have given me pleasure, but in the second I found some traces of carelessness, which I will point out to you when I come home. You must endeavour to speak better, then you will also write better. Your letters, my dear little king of the Moors, also called Paul Hermann, were the best of all, without a single mistake and beautifully short. I praise you in good earnest for your conduct, of which Mother, Rebecca and Fanny give such a charming account. I wonder where I shall get the goats for you.

The eldest child, Fanny Cäcilie, was born on 14th November 1805, and was pronounced by her mother to have 'Bach fugue fingers'; next came Jakob Ludwig Felix on 3rd February 1809, and then Rebecka on 11th April 1811. The family were still living in Hamburg, but as the result of its occupation by the French they left it in 1812 and went to Berlin, where the youngest child, Paul, was born on 30th October 1813. At this time Abraham and Leah were still Jews by religion; Leah's brother, however, had become a Christian, and had taken the name of

4

Bartholdy. For this he was cursed and cast off by his mother, who only became reconciled to him many years later through her grand-daughter Fanny. It may well have been at the advice of his brother-in-law that Abraham decided that his children should be brought up in the Christian faith; they were all baptized under the surname Mendelssohn-Bartholdy, and subsequently Abraham and Leah also became Christians.

Fanny and Felix soon began to show their musical gifts, and when the family paid a visit to Paris in 1816 they were given piano lessons by Madame Bigot, a gifted and stimulating teacher. On their return to Germany education, musical and otherwise, began on a formidable scale; only on Sundays were the children allowed the rare luxury of getting up later than five o'clock in the morning. For literary subjects they went to Karl Heyse, father of the writer, for the piano to Ludwig Berger, for the violin to Henning, and for harmony and composition to Carl Zelter. Of these men it was Zelter who played the most important part in Mendelssohn's career. He was a prolific composer, and his settings of Goethe, though they seem for the most part rather elementary to us now, were much admired by the poet himself; eventually it was he who brought about the memorable meeting between Mendelssohn and Goethe. As a teacher he was severe and thorough, and it was probably through his influence that Mendelssohn retained throughout his life a strong streak of conservatism in his approach to music.

By 1820 he and Fanny had both begun to compose; from her father's point of view it would have been unthinkable for Fanny to become a professional musician, but she remained throughout her life an able and enthusiastic amateur. Several of her songs are included in Felix's Op. 8 and Op. 9; one of these, a setting of Heine's *Verlust*, ends unusually on a half-close, echoing the opening phrase:

This would have been written shortly before 1829; in 1830 Felix enclosed in a letter to Fanny a short Song without Words for piano, which ends in a very similar manner, perhaps intentionally. She was less gay and mercurial than her brother and liable at times to lecture him in a serious, elder-sisterly fashion; in an early letter he addresses her as 'my dear coughing Fanny' in reference to the disapproving sounds that she would make before criticizing his compositions. But through his life he was deeply devoted to her, and he never got over the shock of her death.

The year 1820 is a convenient point from which to take stock of Felix's general progress. He had already appeared on the con-cert platform in 1818, playing the piano part of a trio by Woelfl for piano and two horns; in 1819 he had entered the Berlin Singakademie. Most important of all, he had written a con-siderable amount of music, including a Trio for piano and strings, a Sonata for piano and violin, and two for piano solo. A third Sonata, in G minor, was begun in 1820 and finished during the following year; eventually it was published after Mendelssohn's death as Op. 105. Though not very individual, it is extra-ordinarily fluent and accomplished in its technique.

Early in 1821 Weber visited Berlin; Felix met him and was carried away with an enthusiasm for his music that left its mark on much of his own work. It may well be due to this that the compositions of 1821 included two one-act operettas, *Die beiden Pädagogen* and *Soldatenliebschaft*. Another, *Die wandernden Komö-dianten*, was begun in the same year, and a fourth, in three acts, called *Der Onkel aus Boston*, was begun in 1822 and finished in 1823. Much instrumental music was written during these three years, including twelve symphonies for strings.

Meanwhile towards the end of 1821 came one of the most notable events in Mendelssohn's life, his visit to Goethe. This was organized by Zelter who, for all his gruffness and severity, regarded his young pupil with great pride and affection. The prospect of the visit naturally threw the family into great

6

excitement and their letters of exhortation to Felix are amusingly characteristic. His father writes: 'Every time I write to you, my dear boy, I shall remind you to keep a strict watch over yourself; to sit properly and behave nicely, especially at dinner; to speak distinctly and suitably, and try as much as possible to express yourself to the point.' His mother: 'If I could but be a little mouse so as to watch my dear Felix while he is away and see how he comports himself as an independent youth.' His sister Fanny: 'When you are with Goethe, I advise you to open your eyes and ears wide; and after you come home, if you can't repeat every word that fell from his mouth, I will have nothing more to do with you.'

Travelling for the first time without his parents, Felix was taken to Weimar by Zelter. A lively and intelligent child of great personal charm, he met with a warm reception which he described with delightful vividness when writing to his family:

Now stop and listen, all of you. To-day is Tuesday; on Sunday the sun of Weimar—Goethe—arrived. In the morning we went to church and they gave us half of Handel's 100th Psalm. Afterwards I went to the 'Elephant' where I sketched the house of Lucas Cranach. Two hours afterwards Professor Zelter came and said, 'Goethe has come; the old gentleman's come,' and in a minute we were down the steps and in Goethe's house. He was in the garden, and was just coming round the corner. Isn't it strange, dear Father? that was exactly how you met him. He is very kind, but I don't think any of the pictures are like him.

Later in the day Felix astonished the company by his improvisation on a theme given him by Zelter, who commented, with his usual gruffness: 'What goblins and dragons have you been dreaming about, to drive you along so wildly?' He then played many other things, including some Bach fugues and the overture to *Figaro*, and read at sight some manuscripts. He was made much of by Goethe himself and by his daughter-in-law Ottilie von Goethe and her sister Ulrike von Pogwisch, and he showed his sister Fanny's songs to Ottilie, who had a pleasant voice. Goethe, writing to Rellstab, describes the boy as having 'the smallest possible modicum of the phlegmatic, and the maximum of the opposite quality.' He was, however, anxious that 'the little Berliner,' as he was called, should not have his head turned by too many attentions, and at one point complained to Zelter that the women were doing their best to spoil him. The visit lasted longer than had been planned, and it was over a fortnight before Felix returned to his family.

In 1822 he made his second public appearance as a pianist and went with his family for a tour in Switzerland. During this they passed through Frankfort and he there made the acquaintance of the young pianist Ferdinand Hiller, who became one of his closest friends. On their way home the family visited Goethe at Weimar. In addition to the unpublished works already mentioned, the compositions of 1822 include the piano Quartet in C minor, which was begun at Sécheron and finished after the return home, concertos for piano and for violin, of which the latter has been recently performed, three fugues for piano and several choral works. Of these the piano Quartet was the only one to be published, but many of them were performed at the Sunday morning musical gatherings regularly held in the family circle. To be able to hear so many of his own works was an inestimable advantage and helped him to acquire the *savoir faire* and sureness of effect that hardly ever failed him even in the least inspired of his compositions. At the age of thirteen his appearance had become maturer, with shorter hair and less juvenile clothes; he was extremely quick and lively in self-expression, both in words and on paper. His letters are already astonishingly vivid, and if his opinions are sometimes expressed in an over-dogmatic and self-assured manner, this can easily be forgiven in one so young and so gifted. A musical amateur six years his senior, with the pleasing but improbable name of Wilhelm von Boguslavski, wrote to ask for his opinion of his symphony;

Felix's reply, if patronizing, is formidably shrewd for so young a boy and shows a keen sense of musical design and proportion. When writing to Zelter from Switzerland he shows an equally ready pen for the description of scenery. The year 1823 was one of steady progress; three more chamber works were written, the piano Quartet, Op. 2, and the violin Sonata, Op. 4, both in F minor, and a posthumously published string Quartet in E flat, and also the last three of the twelve symphonies for strings, one of which includes parts for triangle, cymbals and drums. Finally his fourth opera, *Der Onkel aus Boston*, was completed. Writing to Goethe on 11th March 1823, Zelter tells of Felix's progress with an emotion that he would seldom have allowed himself to show to the boy in person:

In everything he gains, and even force and power are now hardly wanting; everything comes from within him, and the external things of the day only affect him externally. Imagine my joy, if we survive, to see the boy living in the fulfilment of all that his childhood gives promise of.

Equally enthusiastic is his description of the first performance of *Der Onkel aus Boston*, which took place in February 1824. And after the performance he actually said to Felix, before the whole company: 'My dear boy, from this day you are no longer an apprentice, but an independent member of the brotherhood of musicians. I proclaim you independent in the name of Mozart, Haydn and old father Bach.'

After this success more works followed in rapid succession: the Symphony in C minor, Op. 11, his first for full orchestra, the interesting but unequal Sextet in D for piano and strings and, a more truly individual work than either of these, the *Rondo capriccioso* for piano. There were also two Concertos for two pianos that were never published, the Overture for military band, composed on a visit to Dobberan, on the Baltic, and the third piano Quartet, in B minor, which was completed during the following year and dedicated to Goethe. Apart from the compositions the most important event of the year was the visit of Moscheles to Berlin in October. After a concert of his, at which Hummel was present, there was a supper party in honour of the two musicians at the Mendelssohns' house. Felix was asked to play, but was overcome by sudden and unwonted nervousness, and left the room in tears. Moscheles, however, was so impressed by both his and Fanny's gifts that he gave lessons to both of them until his departure from Berlin.

CHAPTER II

1825–1830

THE events of 1825 were considerably more varied. Henriette Mendelssohn's pupil had now married, and in March Abraham decided to go to Paris to fetch his sister back. He was still uncertain whether, with all his successes, it was wise to allow Felix to become a professional musician, and he therefore took him too, to show him to Cherubini and ask his advice. The results were startlingly successful: Cherubini was a rugged autocrat with a reputation for withering sarcasm, but on hearing a not particularly good performance of Felix's recently completed piano Quartet in B minor, he said, with surprising amiability: 'Ce garçon est riche; il fera bien; il fait déjà bien, mais il dépense trop de son argent, il met trop d'étoffe dans son habit.' Halévy, who was not present and had himself frequently suffered from Cherubini's tongue, was incredulous when he heard what had happened. Felix in his turn described Cherubini as 'an extinct volcano, still throwing out occasional sparks and flashes, but quite covered with ashes and stones.' He composed a *Kyrie* for voices and orchestra by which he set great store; evidently he was determined in this work to meet Cherubini on his own contrapuntal ground, and it is regrettable that it has not survived. He met many musicians in Paris, including Rossini and Meyerbeer, but the general musical atmosphere sent him into a frenzy of Teutonic patriotism. He heard Auber's *Léocadie*, which he criticized with great severity, and was, not unnaturally, horrified to find that the musical public did not know a note of *Fidelio* and regarded Bach as 'a mere full-bottomed wig powdered with nothing but learning. He continues:

The other day, at Kalkbrenner's request, I played Bach's organ Preludes in E minor and A minor. The people thought them both sweetly pretty, and somebody remarked that the beginning of the A minor Prelude bore a striking resemblance to a duet of Monsigny's—everything danced before my eyes.

A sisterly rebuke from Fanny for his intolerance drew from him an even more indignant tirade, which he himself described as an *allegro feroce*. On his way back from Paris he visited Goethe at Weimar; the dedication to him of the B minor piano Quartet gave great pleasure.

He had by this time developed greatly as a composer: the scherzo of the B minor Quartet and the *Rondo capriccioso* show for the first time the wayward, fairylike brilliance that is so essentially characteristic of him, and the *Seven Characteristic Pieces*, Op. 7, which probably date from 1825, show that he could write in a contrapuntal idiom which is not simply an imitation of Bach or Handel. His fifth opera, *The Wedding of Camacho*,[1] though pleasant, is less striking in quality, but to this same eventful year belong the vigorous and exhilarating *Capriccio* in F sharp minor for piano and, better still, the Octet, which remains his finest chamber work. At about the same time he made a translation of Terence's *Andria* as a present for his teacher Karl Heyse. During the course of the year the family moved to No. 3 Leipzigerstrasse, a large and attractive property just outside Berlin which remained in their possession till after Felix's death. During the next few years the family circle was remarkably happy. The two younger children, Rebecka and Paul, though less gifted than Fanny and Felix, were developing into charming personalities; Felix became a student at Berlin University, and was composing with enthusiasm. The string Quintet in A, Op. 18, was written in 1826, but published some years later with a different second movement; the interesting and unduly neglected piano Sonata in E, Op. 6, dates from the same period and, best of all, there was

[1] Gamacho in Cervantes's *Don Quixote*, from which he took the subject.

the overture to *A Midsummer Night's Dream*, which had its first performance in the open air at Stettin in 1827. Meanwhile *The Wedding of Camacho* was submitted to Spontini, who was the musical director of the Berlin Royal Opera; Felix showed a keen interest in the stage, and this was fostered by his friendship with Eduard Devrient, the singer and actor. A flood of intrigues and worries followed; Spontini was not particularly generous-minded towards his juniors, and his speech to Felix after reading the score: 'Mon ami, il vous faut des idées grandes, grandes comme cette coupole,' referring to the dome of the synagogue, did not give pleasure. Eventually the opera was performed, once only, on 29th April 1827; after this Blum, the tenor, fell ill. It was well received, but the whole incident left Felix with a sense of disappointment. He bitterly resented a hostile criticism of the work in the *Schnellpost*, but at the same time he seems to have felt that the music, now nearly two years old, represented a phase he had since outgrown; before the end of the performance he had left the theatre and Devrient had to appear in his place. He made no attempt to press for a second performance, and his experiences over the production left him with a lingering resentment towards Berlin that lasted till the end of his life. The brilliant success of the previous years of his life probably made it particularly hard for him to put up with anything approaching a setback; also he had felt very deeply the death of his friend August Hanstein, at whose bedside he wrote the fine piano Fugue in E minor afterwards included in Op. 35.

The Mendelssohn family was now the centre of a large circle of friends, varied and interesting in character. Devrient, the singer, and Hiller, the pianist, have already been mentioned: they both wrote memoirs of Felix. Devrient was closely associated with him over tne performance of Bach's Passion according to St. Matthew a few years later, and remained on very friendly terms with him throughout his life. His memoir is of great interest, affectionate but not blindly hero-worshipping, and his views on

his music are worth recording. As a singer and a man of the
theatre he felt all along that opera was the medium most suited
to Mendelssohn's genius; he admired *St. Paul*, but was less
enthusiastic about *Elijah*, and he felt in general that, in the later
works, his admiration for Bach was impairing his true individuality. With most of this it is difficult to agree now; there
is certainly a loss of spontaneity in some of the later works, but
they are also less contrapuntal than the earlier, a fact noted with
approval by Grove and H. F. Chorley. When writing for the
stage he was certainly capable of portraying atmosphere with
wonderful imaginativeness, as in the *Midsummer Night's Dream*
music, and some of *Loreley*, but it is doubtful whether he had
either the emotional range or the power of character-drawing to
become a really great writer of opera. Hiller's memoir is of later
date and on the whole of less value, though the letters are interesting.
His intercourse with Mendelssohn was less continuous than
Devrient's, and towards the end of 1843 there was a misunder-
standing between the two men that was never cleared up, and
they did not meet again. A musician of a very different type
who also frequented the Mendelssohn household at that time was
A. B. Marx, the author of solid but rather tendentious theoretical
works. Abraham Mendelssohn regarded him from the first with
some suspicion, but Felix was much stimulated by his views in
general, and in particular by his enthusiasm for Beethoven: later,
however, there was a quarrel, after which Marx's influence faded
away. A far more lasting friendship was with Karl Klingemann,
a diplomat who in a few years' time was sent to London. He
was a sensitive and sympathetic personality to whom all the
family were much attached, and his departure for London was
greatly regretted by them. He is seen from another angle in the
letters of Fanny and Sophia Horsley, collected in R. B. Gotch's
book *Mendelssohn and his Friends in Kensington*; his earnest demeanour and somewhat ambassadorial manners appear to have
been regarded by the young ladies with good-natured amusement.

The music written by Felix in 1827 gives an interesting indication of his various tastes and enthusiasms. The Fugue in E minor and the motet *Tu es Petrus*, written as a birthday present for Fanny, show, in different ways, his attraction towards counterpoint resulting from his love for Bach. Meanwhile he was becoming increasingly interested in the later works of Beethoven; this is most evident in the A minor Quartet, Op. 13, but it can also be seen, to a lesser extent, in parts of the E major piano Sonata and, in a more diluted form, in the less interesting Sonata in B flat. The keyboard writing in the sonatas is sometimes reminiscent of Weber; on the other hand the influence of Mozart, so noticeable in the earlier works, is now far less in evidence, *The Wedding of Camacho* being the last in which it is still important.

During the latter part of 1827 Felix seems to have recovered his spirits. In the summer he went on an excursion to the Harz mountains, visiting various places. One of the pleasantest results of this was his meeting with Thibaut, who was Professor of Law at Heidelberg, and an enthusiastic admirer of the Italian composers of the sixteenth century, particularly Palestrina. He introduced Felix to these, and Felix retaliated by introducing Thibaut to Bach; when they parted Thibaut said to him: 'Farewell, and we will build our friendship on Luis de Victoria and Sebastian Bach, like two lovers who promise each other to look at the moon, and then fancy they are near each other.' *Tu es Petrus*, begun on the tour, was finished on his return home; also, perhaps as a deliberately frivolous contrast, a Toy Symphony modelled on that of Haydn. Klingemann had by this time gone to London; he writes entertainingly to the Mendelssohns, commenting on the size of London, the gloom of the British Sunday, the beauty of the Goltermanns' housemaid, the difficulty of pronouncing the English 'th' and other fascinating topics. Meanwhile Felix had started weekly rehearsals of the St. Matthew Passion, partly in order to shake the opinion of his clerical friend Schubring that Bach's music was nothing but mathematics. The year 1828 was less eventful; two cantatas were composed, one for the Dürer Festival, the other, rather surprisingly, for a congress of scientists, and later in the year came the fine overture inspired by Goethe's twin poems *A Calm Sea* and *A Prosperous Voyage*.

Rehearsals of the Passion had been continuing all through the year, and early in 1829 Devrient was determined to have it performed at the Singakademie. He was longing to sing the part of Christ, and Felix must conduct; therefore there was no time to be lost, as it had already been decided that later in the year Felix was to pay a visit to England. The first problem was to get Zelter's permission, and Devrient has given a very vivid account of this process in his memoir. Of the two young men he had the robuster and less sensitive personality, and was the more confident of the possibility of breaking down Zelter's objections. Together they bearded him; Zelter informed them that the undertaking was quite impossible, that they would find no suitable string players, that better men than they had failed in similar enterprises, that they would have nothing but misery from the choir, and then finally yielded, giving the project his blessing. When they had left the room Devrient, who had played his cards with great skill and determination, exclaimed: 'We have won!' 'Yes, but you are a rascal, an arch-jesuit'; 'Anything you like for the honour of Sebastian Bach.' Eventually the work was given for the first time since Bach's death on 11th March and again on 21st March, Bach's birthday, with the greatest success. 'To think that it should be an actor and a Jew that have given back to the people the greatest Christian work' was Felix's triumphant comment. A week after his departure from Berlin there was a third performance under Zelter.

Felix had undoubtedly achieved a very great personal triumph, but he seems to have been regarded with jealousy by some of the older Berlin musicians, including Spontini, who had tried to prevent the second performance of the Passion and probably still regarded him as an upstart amateur. He left Berlin on 10th April and was accompanied by his father and his sister Rebecka as far as Hamburg; there he was greeted by a farewell letter from Fanny who, a few months before, had become engaged to the painter Wilhelm Hensel. He found the crossing highly unpleasant, but in London his spirits soon revived. Klingemann and the Moscheles couple did all that they could for him, and he was soon plunged in a whirl of musical and social activities. Four days after his arrival he wrote to his family:

London is the grandest and most complicated monster on the face of the earth. How can I compress into one letter what I have been three days seeing? I hardly remember the chief events and yet I must not keep a diary, for then I should see less of life, and that must not be. On the contrary, I want to catch hold of whatever offers itself to me. Things roll and whirl round me and carry me along as in a vortex.

He heard Rossini's *Otello,* with Malibran singing the part of Desdemona, and came into contact with many musicians.

He found the general approach to music in London less learned and critical but more spontaneously enthusiastic than that of Berlin, and it was only natural that he should have revelled in it, especially after the worries and disappointment of *Camacho.* On 25th May he conducted his Symphony in C minor at the Philharmonic Society's concert, substituting for the minuet a beautifully orchestrated version of the scherzo from the Octet. He conducted from the piano, to which he was formally escorted by J. B. Cramer 'like a young lady,' and had an enthusiastic reception, the scherzo being encored. The Symphony was dedicated to the society, of which Felix was soon made an honorary member. After seeing a rather eccentric performance of *Hamlet* by Charles Kemble he wrote to his family that 'there is little poetry in England,' but in general his letters show the warmest appreciation of his surroundings, and, quite apart from his music, his liveliness, charm and many social accomplishments won for him innumerable friends. At the Moscheles' house he met Sigismund von

Neukomm, an industrious but not very inspired musician who had come to London that year, and was to come into contact with Felix subsequently in connection with the Birmingham Festival. He appeared successfully as a pianist, playing one of his own unpublished concertos for two pianos with Moscheles, and, much to his amusement, he was asked to compose a hymn for a festival in Ceylon celebrating the emancipation of the natives. But during these first months in England there was little time for composition, and his family were beginning to fear that he was becoming too deeply immersed in society. Late in July, however, he and Klingemann left London for Edinburgh, and the change of surroundings soon began to stir his imagination. He was much impressed by Edinburgh:

When God Himself takes to panorama-painting, it turns out strangely beautiful. Few of my Switzerland reminiscences can compare to this; everything looks so stern and robust, half enveloped in haze or smoke or fog; moreover there is to be a bagpipe competition to-morrow; many Highlanders came in costume from church, victoriously leading their sweethearts in their Sunday attire and casting magnificent and important looks over the world; with long red beards, tartan plaids, bonnets and feathers, naked knees, and their bagpipes in their hands, they passed quietly along by the half-ruined gray castle on the meadow, where Mary Stuart lived in splendour and saw Rizzio murdered. I feel as if time went at a very rapid pace when I have before me so much that was and so much that is.

He soon formed the idea of composing a 'Scottish' Symphony, and on 30th July 1829, in the ruined chapel of Mary Stuart, he thought of the introduction to the first movement, though it was twelve years before the work was completed. He and Klinge-mann went to visit Sir Walter Scott at Abbotsford, but this seems to have been something of an anticlimax; in Felix's words: 'We found Sir Walter in the act of leaving Abbotsford, stared at him like fools, drove eighty miles and lost a day for the sake of at best one half-hour of superficial conversation.' Whenever they came to a view that took their fancy Felix made a sketch of it and Klingemann wrote a short poem underneath. They went up to the Hebrides, and in one of his letters from there he includes a sketch of what eventually became the opening bars of the *Hebrides* overture. From there they came south, through Glasgow and the Lake District to Liverpool; Klingemann then returned to London and Felix went to Wales. His first recorded impressions of this country are of its native music, which his essentially urbane temperament found highly distasteful:

No national music for me! Ten thousand devils take all nationality! Now I am in Wales and, dear me, a harper sits in the hall of every reputed inn, playing incessantly so-called national melodies; that is to say, most infamous, vulgar, out-of-tune trash, with a hurdy-gurdy going on at the same time. It is distracting and has given me a toothache already. Scotch bagpipes, Swiss cow-horns, Welsh harps, all playing the Huntsmen's Chorus with hideously improvised variations—then their beautiful singing in the hall—altogether their music is beyond conception.

However, he settled down at Coed-du very happily with his hosts, the Taylor family, and for the three daughters he wrote his three Fantasias or Caprices, Op. 16, the first being inspired by a bunch of carnations and roses, the second by some small trumpet-shaped flowers that one of the girls wore in her hair, and the third by a stream. Meanwhile several larger works were taking shape in his mind: the string Quartet in E flat, Op. 12, which was finished before the end of the year, and the Fantasia or Scotch Sonata for piano in F sharp minor, Op. 28, which is commonly supposed to have been composed in 1833, but must be of earlier date, as he played it to Goethe in 1830. He was also working at an organ piece for Fanny's wedding, and the delightful operetta *Son and Stranger*, to a libretto by Klingemann, for his parents' silver wedding. Meanwhile in the background were the *Hebrides* overture and the 'Reformation' and 'Scottish' Symphonies.

He was back in London early in September and had hoped to be in Berlin in time for Fanny's wedding on 3rd October, but his plans were upset by a carriage accident as the result of which one of his legs was seriously hurt. He had to stay in bed for two months and was nursed with great care by Klingemann. When he was able to move about he stayed with the English composer Attwood, who had been a pupil of Mozart; at his house he found a full score of Weber's *Euryanthe* and had the satisfaction of discovering that he had guessed correctly about the scoring of a certain passage. Though much disappointed at missing his sister's wedding, he wrote with great appreciation of the kindness of his friends in England and described his last fortnight in London as 'the happiest and richest that I have enjoyed there.' Before leaving he had finished *Son and Stranger*; for one number, 'Die Blumenglocken mit hellem Schein,' the composer and the librettist decided to change places, Felix writing the words and Klingemann the music. The part of Schulz was written for Wilhelm Hensel, now married to Fanny; as he was tone-deaf the part was written on one note only, which however he failed to find at the first performance on 26th December, despite the fact that, according to Devrient, 'it was blown and whistled to him on every side.' Shortly before the performance there was a disturbing incident: Devrient, who was to sing the chief baritone part, was summoned to a concert at the crown prince's, which threatened to prevent him from returning in time for the performance of the operetta. This threw Felix into a state of almost hysterical agitation, and he alarmed the company by beginning to talk incoherently, in English, and only recovered after twelve hours' sleep. Eventually it was arranged that Devrient should be allowed to leave the court concert in time to take his part in the performance of *Son and Stranger*, which was a great success; but the incident showed how difficult Felix found it to keep his equanimity if things did not go exactly as he wished.

CHAPTER III

1831–1833

MEANWHILE Felix was working hard upon a more serious and less spontaneous work, the 'Reformation' Symphony, which was intended for the tercentenary of the Augsburg Protestant Confession. At this time there were frequent arguments in the family circle about the political situation in France; according to Devrient Felix's views, compared with those of his very conservative father and brother-in-law, seemed positively revolutionary. Early in 1830 the University of Berlin founded a new professorship of music, which it was hoped Felix would take. However, he declined it, probably with wisdom, as he was too highly strung and volatile to be a good teacher; at his suggestion the professorship was given to Marx. It had been decided that he should go on a tour to Italy. But for the second time his plans were delayed by illness; his younger sister Rebecka caught the measles. Felix was very reluctant to start without seeing her, and was almost triumphant when he too caught the disease. Eventually, however, he set out on 19th May; he was accompanied by his father as far as Dessau, where he stayed with his friend Schubring, who some years later arranged the text of *Elijah*. From there he went on to Weimar, where he paid a very happy visit to Goethe. He was warmly welcomed by the poet and his family; he played them some of his piano works, including the *Fantasia* in F sharp minor, and the three pieces that he had written in Wales, and also Beethoven's C minor Symphony, of which Goethe said: 'That causes no emotion; it is merely strange and grandiose.' His

portrait was painted there and he sent to Fanny his recently completed symphony, asking for advice about its title:

Try to collect opinions as to the title I ought to select: 'Reformation'
Symphony, 'Confession' Symphony, Symphony for a Church Festival,
'Juvenile' Symphony or whatever you like. Write to me about it, and
instead of all the stupid suggestions, send me one clever one; but I also
want to hear all the nonsensical ones that are sure to be produced on
the occasion.

His next stopping-place was Munich: Marx, who met him
there, wrote to Fanny a glowing account of his great social success
there. He seems to have been the centre of social life, and to have
indulged in a certain amount of light-hearted and inconclusive
flirtation. Meanwhile Fanny was expecting a child; on 14th June
Felix sent her the little Song without Words already mentioned,
and on the 26th another to celebrate the birth of the boy. This
is the fiery and spirited piece in B flat minor that later appeared
in a slightly altered form as Op. 30, No. 2. From Munich he
proceeded through various places, and from Linz he wrote to
his mother an amusing account of various minor mishaps on the
journey. He went through Vienna to Pressburg, where he saw
the coronation of the King of Hungary, and at last, on 10th
October, he arrived at Venice, where he wrote the Gondola
Song, Op. 19, No. 6. 'Italy at last. And what I have all my
life considered as the greatest possible felicity is now begun, and
I am basking in it.' He wrote with the greatest enthusiasm of
the pictures that he saw, especially Titian's 'Entombment'; of
much of the music he heard he was severely critical. He writes
indignantly to Zelter:

As I was earnestly contemplating the enchanting evening landscape
with its trees, and angels among the boughs, the organ commenced.
The first sound was quite in harmony with my feelings: but the second,
third, and in fact all the rest, quickly roused me from my reveries and
sent me straight home, for the man was playing in church, and during
divine service, and in front of respectable people thus:

with the 'Martyrdom of St. Peter' actually close beside him.

As on his French travels five years before, he was shocked by the general ignorance of serious music, not only in Italy, but in Munich and Vienna.

Moreover, not one of the best pianoforte players there, male or female, ever played a note of Beethoven, and when I hinted that he and Mozart were not to be despised, they said: 'So you are an admirer of classical music?'—'Yes,' said I.

From Venice he went to Florence and from there to Rome, where he stayed from 1st November 1830 to 10th April 1831. His life here is fully and vividly described in his letters. He was pleased to find that Goethe, many years before, had arrived in Rome for the first time on 1st November; he was deeply thrilled on seeing the originals of Italian paintings of which he had hitherto only seen copies. There were meetings with many distinguished people: Thorvaldsen the sculptor, Horace Vernet the painter, Baron de Bunsen the diplomat, at whose house he improvised very successfully before a number of Roman musicians. But he felt the lack of a friend in whom he could confide about his own work; there was nobody who could take the place of Klingemann in London. Meanwhile at home Abraham Mendelssohn had become increasingly difficult and irritable; Felix, who in the past had had differences with him about the music of Beethoven, wrote a sensible and sympathetic letter to his brother and sisters, urging them to be as tactful and tolerant as possible towards their father. Towards the end of November the pope, Pius VIII, was seriously ill; Felix commented caustically on the casual attitude of the Italians, whose one anxiety was that the pope might be tactless enough to die in February and so upset the Carnival festivities. To his father he wrote a long and affectionate birthday letter enclosing the opening bars of an unfinished piano piece—rather pompous in character, it must be admitted. The pope died on 1st December, and his successor, Gregory XVI, was elected early in the following February. By a happy chance the festivities that followed coincided with Felix's birthday, and he wrote an exuberant description of them, pretending that the whole thing had been arranged for his special benefit. In March Berlioz arrived in Rome; he was in a state of extreme agitation owing to the erratic conduct of his fiancée, Camille Moke, but he liked Felix immediately and wrote of him with great appreciation. On the other hand, to Felix's fastidious and classically trained mind Berlioz's music seemed merely untidy, and his manners merely theatrical, and he wrote to his mother with a regrettable lack of generosity:

You say, my dear mother, that Berlioz must have a fixed aim in his art; but this is far from being my opinion. I believe he wishes to be married. . . . I really cannot stand his obtrusive enthusiasm, and the gloomy despondency he assumes before ladies—this stereotyped genius in black and white; and if he were not a Frenchman (and it is always pleasant to associate with them, as they have invariably something interesting to say), it would be beyond endurance.

His opinion of Berlioz's music remained unchanged, but his behaviour to him was always friendly and considerate.

He wrote to his family and to Zelter elaborate descriptions of the liturgical music that he heard in the Sistine Chapel during Holy Week, and the number of quotations in these show how remarkable was his memory. His tastes are interesting: plainsong merely irritated him, and his liking for the intonation for the Credo was clearly due to its association in his mind with Bach's B minor Mass. On the other hand he was deeply impressed by Palestrina's Lamentations and Improperia, and he had sufficient historical sense to realize that the copious ornamentation with which much of the music was sung could not be an ancient tradition, as was commonly said, but had crept in at a quite recent date. Antiquity in itself made no special appeal to him, and he was more deeply moved by landscapes than by ancient buildings: 'The sea lay between the islands, and the rocks, covered with vegetation, bent over it then just as they do now. These are the antiquities that interest me and are much more suggestive than crumbling mason-work.' The first version of the *Hebrides* over-ture had been completed in December, but it was revised in 1832; in November he had finished his setting of Psalm CXV, the 'Scottish' and 'Italian' Symphonies were occupying him, and in 1831 he wrote the fine setting of Goethe's *Die Erste Walpurgisnacht*, which was revised later and eventually published as Op. 60. Most of April and May were spent at Naples; then, after returning to Rome for a short time, he began to travel gradually homewards. A project for visiting Sicily was dis-couraged by his father. He went through Genoa and Florence to Milan, where he stayed for a week. The commandant there was General Ertmann, to whose wife Dorothea Beethoven had dedicated his Sonata in A major, Op. 101. Felix wrote to his family a charming account of his visit to them. She played two Beethoven sonatas, to the delight of the general, who had not heard her play for a long time, and Felix replied with the Trio in B flat, Op. 97, singing the string parts. He also met at Milan Mozart's son Karl, to whom he took a great liking. About this time he had an interesting correspondence with Devrient, who was already worried because he felt that Felix was writing too much choral music under the influence of Bach and could main-tain his individuality more by writing operas. Felix in his reply dwells on the difficulty of finding the right libretto. His moral-izing, essentially Teutonic approach to music, that was so much in evidence on his first visit to Paris, continued throughout his life, especially where opera was concerned. On a later occasion he wrote from Paris criticizing in a censorious and rather priggish manner the libretti of *Robert le Diable* and *Fra Diavolo*, and it is probable that, whatever libretto he ultimately chose, this attitude of mind would have prevented him from being a musical dramatist of the calibre of Mozart or Verdi.

From Milan he proceeded to Switzerland; the letters written from there are full of vivid descriptions of the scenery and of organs on which he played. In a letter to Goethe he gives a very amusing account of a performance of Schiller's *Wilhelm Tell*. Eventually he arrived at Munich, where he remained for some time. The piano Concerto in G minor, hastily written, as he himself admitted, was played at a concert on 17th October, in company with the Symphony in C minor and the *Midsummer Night's Dream* overture. He was commissioned to write an opera for the Munich theatre, and he went to Düsseldorf to consult with Karl Immermann about a libretto. They agreed on *The Tempest*, but Felix was not attracted by Immermann's libretto, and nothing came of it. If the project had been carried out, the results might well have been interesting. The music dealing with Ariel and with the sea would almost certainly have been admirable, the love music for Ferdinand and Miranda would have been suitably restrained in its lyricism, and the more nagging moods of Prospero might have been all too vividly portrayed; whether Felix would have been so successful with the solemnity of his final speech, the villainy of Antonio or the grotesque pathos of Caliban may be doubted. Still less likely is it that he would have succeeded with the *Nibelungen*, on which he was at one time planning an opera. On his way to Düsseldorf he visited Frankfort, where he received the news of the engagement of his sister Rebecka to Gustav Dirichlet and also of the death of his Aunt Henriette.

The larger compositions written during this period of travel have already been mentioned, but there were many others. Some songs were composed in Switzerland, including the beautiful setting of Goethe's *Die Liebende schreibt*; also the first Song without Words from Book I, which is one of the best of his short pieces.

The three Motets for women's voices and organ, Op. 39, were written in Rome, and also the Hymn *Verleib' uns Frieden* and the three choral pieces, Op. 23.

In December 1831 he went to Paris for the second time, remaining there till the following April. As might be expected, he was soon plunged in a whirl of social engagements of various kinds. He renewed his friendship with Cherubini and made many new friends, including Habeneck, Ole Bull, Chopin, Liszt and Meyerbeer. He did not approve of Liszt's compositions; those of Chopin attracted him more, though sometimes he found them too wayward for his liking. He was on thoroughly friendly terms with Habeneck and Meyerbeer, though on one occasion he altered his mode of hairdressing in order to avoid being mistaken for the latter. His closest friendship during this period was with Hiller, who has described it vividly in his memoir. They had many arguments together, especially on the subject of Italian and French music, on which Felix was highly critical. He could, however, criticize his own compatriots as well and remarked, with a touch of shrewdness, that Handel might be said to have different musical drawers for his choruses, one labelled 'warlike,' another 'heathen,' a third 'religious,' and so forth. He had some public successes, playing Beethoven's G major Concerto at the Conservatoire under Habeneck, and hearing his Octet played, very unsuitably, at a funeral mass in memory of Beethoven. But there was also a severe disappointment: the 'Reformation' Symphony was to have been performed by Habeneck, but after a rehearsal the orchestra took a dislike to it as having too much counterpoint and too little melody, and the performance never took place. He was also much affected by the death, in January, of his friend Eduard Rietz, the violinist; in his memory was written the *adagio* that eventually became the second movement of the string Quintet in A. In March came another personal loss in the death of Goethe, which he felt very deeply. On the whole it was as a personality, a performer and

an organizer rather than as a composer that he made his mark in
Paris. When listening to a performance of his own A minor
Quartet, Op. 13, he overheard a member of the audience say:
'Il y a cela dans une de ses symphonies'—'Qui?'—'Beethoven,
l'auteur de ce quatuor.' It was some time before he could get
over the disappointment of the rejection of the 'Reformation' Symphony. With his great love for Bach he set special store by his
more contrapuntal works, for which Paris seemed to have no use.

Owing to a slight attack of cholera he stayed there longer than
he had intended; in April he arrived in London and wrote:
'I wish I could only describe how happy I feel to be here once
more; how much I like everything, and how gratified I am by
the kindness of old friends.' In an earlier letter, written from
Naples, he says of London: 'That smoky nest is fated for ever
to be my favourite residence.' This second English visit was
shorter and less eventful than the first, but he enjoyed it greatly;
Klingemann, the Moscheles and the Attwoods were still there,
and he became very friendly with the Horsley family, with whom
he kept in touch for the rest of his life. The *Capriccio brillante*
in B minor for piano and orchestra was written and performed
during this visit; the only sadness was the death of Zelter on
15th May. This was not only a deep personal grief, but also led
to a practical problem, as it left vacant the conductorship of the
Singakademie at Berlin. Felix had for some time felt uncertain
about his position in Berlin; when in Paris he had said in a letter
to his father that it was the only city in Germany with which he
was unacquainted, and now, after Zelter's death, he wrote in a
similar vein:

I do not know how I shall get on in Berlin, or whether I shall be able
to remain there; that is, whether I shall be able to enjoy the same
facilities for work, and progress, that are offered to me in other places.
The only house that I know in Berlin is our own, and I feel certain
I shall be quite happy there; but I must also be in a position to be actively
employed, and this I shall discover when I return.

He returned to Berlin in July; the Singakademie was temporarily in the hands of Zelter's assistant, Rungenhagen. Felix would gladly have filled Zelter's post, either on his own or in conjunction with Rungenhagen. But the idea of sharing the post with Mendelssohn did not appeal to Rungenhagen, who was an older man and felt that he had a strong claim to hold it under the same conditions as Zelter. At this point Mendelssohn would probably have been wiser to withdraw his claim, but owing largely to the misguided zeal of Devrient he did not, and a long period of delay and suspense followed. At last the election took place in January 1833, and the voting went heavily in favour of Rungenhagen. As a result the whole of the Mendelssohn family withdrew in dudgeon from the Singakademie, and Felix's attitude towards Berlin became still less cordial. Luckily there were distractions; he had been commissioned in November 1832 by the London Philharmonic Society to compose 'a symphony, an overture and a vocal piece' for one hundred guineas, and the first of these was to be the 'Italian' Symphony. He had been working at this for some time, and during the previous autumn he had been through acute misgivings over it. However, by April he felt satisfied, and towards the end of the month he took it in person to England, with two overtures. The identity of these seems uncertain, but it is thought that they were the *Hebrides* in its revised version and the earlier 'Trumpet' Overture. The vocal piece, the concert aria *Infelice*, was not written till 1834. The Symphony was performed at the Philharmonic concert on 13th May, and the programme also included Mozart's D minor Concerto, played with great success by Felix. In a few days he left London for Düsseldorf. He had been engaged to conduct the Lower Rhine Festival there, and before his last visit to England he had been there for a short time to make the preliminary arrangements.

The Festival began on 26th May, and Abraham Mendelssohn came to it and described it vividly in his letters. The two largest works were Handel's *Israel in Egypt* and Beethoven's 'Pastoral'

Symphony; Felix's own work was represented by the 'Trumpet' Overture, which had always been a special favourite of his father. It was the greatest public success that he had yet had in Germany, and it resulted in his being asked to become regular musical director at Düsseldorf for three years, for 600 thaler a year. This appointment, which was to start on 1st October 1833, he accepted with alacrity, and he spent the intervening time in London, taking his father with him. Abraham enjoyed the social side of the visit but could not quite share his son's immense enthusiasm for England. He wrote in a gently satirical manner about the climate:

This morning at fourteen minutes past nine the sun was just powerful enough to give a yellow tinge to the mist, and the air was just like the smoke of a great fire. 'A fine morning,' said my barber (here called hairdresser). 'Is it?' asked I. 'Yes, a very fine morning,' and so I learnt what a fine summer morning is like here.

Felix's 'Trumpet' Overture was performed at a Philharmonic concert on 10th June, and he played the organ at St. Paul's Cathedral. By a curious coincidence the journey home was again delayed by an accident, Abraham injuring his shin, and it was not till 25th August that they were able to leave for Berlin. Felix was much concerned over his father and nursed him with the utmost devotion. Abraham puzzled his family by announcing that he was bringing home with him a promising and attractive young painter called Alphonse Lovie; this, however, turned out to be Felix, whose unexpected arrival was received with the greatest delight. By this time Rebecka and Gustav Dirichlet were married and living with the Mendelssohns in Berlin; their eldest child was born in July. Paul had gone to England in 1831, but returned early in 1834 and worked in his uncle Joseph Mendelssohn's bank. After his surprise arrival in Berlin Felix spent a few very happy days with his family before leaving for Düsseldorf.

CHAPTER IV

1834–1837

FELIX went to Düsseldorf determined to raise the standard in both ecclesiastical and theatrical music, but, as so often happens to reformers, he soon found more difficulties than he had expected. He first turned his attention to the church music, deciding that 'no appropriate epithet exists for the music which has hitherto been given here.' He introduced works by Palestrina, Leo, Lassus and others. This was not particularly well received by the citizens of Düsseldorf, but worse was to follow. At the theatre he announced a series of 'classical' performances, beginning with *Don Giovanni*; this involved a raising of the prices, and there were disturbances on the first night. Felix insisted on a public apology, which was eventually made, and for a time things ran smoothly. But as a result of the trouble his relations with Immermann became less and less cordial, and he eventually resigned from the theatrical part of his post. It is interesting to compare his determination and inflexibility on musical matters with the extreme caution and deference with which at the same period he wrote to his father on an entirely different matter:

I must now ask your advice on a particular subject; I have long wished to ride here, and when Lessing lately bought a horse he advised me strongly to do the same. I think the regular exercise would do me good—this is in favour of the scheme; but against it, there is the possibility of its becoming an inconvenient and even tyrannical custom, as I should think it my duty to ride, if possible, every day; then I also wished to ask you whether you don't think it rather too genteel for me, at my years, to have a horse of my own? In short I am undecided and beg now, as I have often done before, to hear your opinion, by which mine will be regulated.

31

All through his life he felt an almost religious devotion to his family in general, and in particular to his father as head of the family.

Meanwhile a new and important musical project began to take shape. During his last visit to Paris in 1832 he had been com-missioned to compose an oratorio for the Cäcilien-Verein at Frankfort dealing with St. Paul. It had been decided that the libretto should be arranged by Marx and that Felix in his turn should produce a libretto on the subject of Moses for Marx. This he did, but Marx not only rejected it but also decided not to undertake *St. Paul* because he disliked the idea of introducing chorales. After this display of obstructionism it is hardly sur-prising that Felix's affection for him cooled rapidly, and eventually they drifted apart. Felix started to prepare the libretto of *St. Paul* himself, with assistance from Schubring and other friends. The music was begun in March 1834, but was not finished for nearly two years. In May he went to the Lower Rhine Festival at Aachen, where there was a pleasant meeting with Chopin and Hiller. After praising their piano playing in a letter to his mother, he adds characteristically:

Both, however, rather toil in the Parisian spasmodic and impassioned style, too often losing sight of time and sobriety and of true music; I, again, do so perhaps too little, thus we all three mutually learn something and improve each other, while I feel rather like a schoolmaster, and they a little like 'mirliflors' or 'incroyables.'

Hiller has described vividly how all three of them went to a party at which Chopin for a long time sat silent and unnoticed; the moment he began to play, however, everyone else in the room was forgotten.

Although Felix's position with regard to the Düsseldorf theatre was now honorary, he was still concerned with the engagement of singers, which he found a very worrying and uncongenial occupation. Devrient, who was far more experienced in the ways of the theatre, did all he could to help him, but Felix's letters are full of a sense of strain and irritation: 'Fräulein Grosser will roast in the musical inferno for turning her poetic soul away from us for 500 thaler. How miserable the devils are we know from *Robert le Diable*, and there it will be still worse.' A new theatre was to be opened at Düsseldorf, and in August Felix went to Berlin to interview the singers Devrient had collected for him. This resulted in much sordid bargaining and double-dealing; eventually he returned to Düsseldorf in October, and the theatre was opened with Immermann as director. But the relations between him and Felix, which had been steadily deteriorating, were now strained to breaking-point, and within a month's time Felix broke off all connections with the theatre. There is no doubt that he had had much to put up with, but even Devrient, who felt the greatest affection for him, admits that he did not handle the difficult situations well, largely because he had been so accustomed to having his own way in everything. His father evidently took the same view, and summed up the position with considerable shrewdness in a letter written to Felix some time later:

But on your return to Düsseldorf, after wisely refusing to undertake another journey for the purpose of making engagements for the theatre, instead of persevering in your duties in this sense, and getting rid of all 'odiosa,' you allowed yourself to be overwhelmed by them; and as they naturally became most obnoxious to you, instead of quietly striving to remedy them, and thus gradually to get rid of them, you at one leap extricated yourself, and by so doing you undeniably subjected yourself to the imputation of fickleness and unsteadiness, and made a decided enemy of a man whom at all events policy should have taught you not to displease; and most probably offended and lost the friendliness of many members of the 'Comité' also, among whom there are, no doubt, most respectable people. If I view this matter incorrectly, then teach me a better mode of judging.

Luckily all this unpleasantness did not keep Felix from composition: in addition to *St. Paul*, which was slowly taking shape, the concert aria *Infelice*, the Rondo in E flat for piano and orchestra and, better than either of these, the *Melusine* overture. He was impelled to write this by acute irritation with the overture to Conradin Kreutzer's opera on this subject, and he considered it one of his best works; he was therefore suitably annoyed by the purple journalistic fantasies that it inspired in the *Musikalische Zeitung*. He remained at Düsseldorf, but early in 1835 he was offered the conductorship of the Gewandhaus concerts at Leipzig. To this he replied with great caution, which may have been to some extent the result of his disagreeable experiences at Düsseldorf, but it also showed an admirable scrupulousness and anxiety to avoid treading on the heels of any other musician. Eventually the offer was accepted, but the appointment was not taken up till October. Before that he conducted the Lower Rhine Festival at Cologne, the chief works being Beethoven's eighth Symphony and Handel's *Solomon*, of which he had made an abridged edition when in Italy. After the festival the committee presented him with Arnold's edition of Handel's works, which gave him great satisfaction. The festival was attended by his parents, sisters and brothers-in-law, and afterwards his parents returned with him to Düsseldorf. Some anxious times followed; his mother fell ill, which delayed their return to Berlin, and on their journey home, on which Felix accompanied them, Abraham was taken ill at Cassel. Felix stayed with them at Berlin till the end of August and he then left for Leipzig.

He settled there very happily and found the atmosphere far more congenial than that of Düsseldorf. Shortly after his arrival he had a welcome visit from Chopin, and about the same time he made the acquaintance of Robert Schumann and of his future wife, Clara Wieck. Felix played some of *St. Paul* to Chopin, who retaliated with his latest *études* and concerto; it was, in Felix's words, 'as if a Cherokee and a Kaffir had met to converse.' There was also a very welcome visit from Moscheles. His first concert included *A Calm Sea and a Prosperous Voyage*;

on two later occasions Moscheles played. The Dirichlets passed through Leipzig and took Felix and Moscheles with them to Berlin for a short visit, where there was much pleasant gaiety. Abraham Mendelssohn was by now quite blind, but apart from that his health had given no cause for serious anxiety. It was therefore a terrible shock to Felix when, shortly after his return to Leipzig, Hensel came to break to him the news of his father's sudden death. He at once went to his mother in Berlin, arriving on 22nd November, three days after Abraham's death. He had been taken ill the previous night, but the doctors had sensed no immediate danger; his passing, for all its suddenness, appears to have been peaceful and painless.

He soon had to return to Leipzig, and his chief desire was to finish *St. Paul*. His father had always been anxious for him to write an oratorio, and he felt that he was fulfilling a special duty in completing it. Originally it had been hoped that it would be ready to be performed at Frankfort in November, but it was not finished in time, and the illness of Schelble, the conductor of the Cäcilien-Verein, put a further obstacle to its being performed there. It was however accepted for the Düsseldorf Festival of 1836. Meanwhile the musical activities of Leipzig continued satisfactorily; in January Felix played Mozart's D minor Concerto, with very effective cadenzas, and in February Beethoven's ninth Symphony was performed very successfully. The leader of the orchestra was Ferdinand David, who was a most loyal and helpful friend to Felix. In March the University conferred on him the degree of Doctor of Philosophy. *St. Paul* was given at the Düsseldorf Festival in May; it was an undoubted success, though possibly less sensational than Felix had hoped. An awkward moment near the beginning, when one of the false witnesses missed his lead, was saved by Fanny, who was singing among the contraltos and surreptitiously gave him his cue. Soon after the festival Felix went to Frankfort and was upset by a rather patronizing criticism of *St. Paul*. But there is no doubt that, quite apart from *St. Paul,* the festival had been a great personal success for him and helped to lift him from the depression into which the death of his father had plunged him. For some time his family had been anxious about his state of mind, and Fanny had often expressed a wish that he would marry; Abraham had once said to Devrient: 'I am afraid that Felix's censoriousness will prevent his getting a wife as well as a libretto,' a speech curiously prophetic of Brahms's much-quoted remark about the difficulties of marriage and of the composition of opera. At Frankfort he conducted the Cäcilien-Verein in place of Schelble, who was still ill, and performed many interesting works, including Bach's *Gottes Zeit* and Handel's *Samson.* Hiller was living at Frankfort, and there was a visit from Rossini, whom Felix had originally met during his first stay in Paris. He thoroughly appreciated his liveliness and exuberance, though, with his usual sensitiveness to criticism, he was not pleased when Rossini pointed out, with some justice, the influence of Domenico Scarlatti on the Capriccio in F sharp minor, Op. 5.

Of greater importance, however, was his meeting with the family of Madame Jeanrenaud, the widow of a clergyman of the French Reformed Church. She was a lively and attractive lady, and for some time it was thought that she herself was the cause of Felix's frequent visits to the house. The real attraction, how-ever, was the second daughter, Cécile, with whom Felix soon fell deeply in love. At first, however, he showed no sign of his feelings, but, in order to test them, he deliberately went away on a visit to Scheveningen; finding them unchanged he returned to Frankfort, proposed and was accepted. Cécile was ten years younger than Felix but had heard of him in her childhood; she had, however, pictured him as an irritable old gentleman, sitting at the piano in a satin cap and playing nothing but fugues. She herself was a less vivacious personality than her mother, reserved and rather elusive, but of great charm, serenity and good sense. For anyone as restless and highly strung as Felix a wife of similar temperament would have been disastrous; Cécile, though not outstandingly gifted in that direction, was musical enough to sympathize with her husband's work and aims, and her calm and unobtrusive goodness was an admirable foil to his mercurial energy. They became formally engaged on 9th September; on 2nd October he resumed his duties at Leipzig. Shortly after this *St. Paul* had its first performance in England, at Liverpool. At Leipzig Sterndale Bennett appeared very successfully with his piano Concerto in C minor, and he and Felix saw much of each other. Knowing of Felix's engagement the directors included in the concert on 12th December the finale of the second act of *Fidelio*, after which Felix extemporized triumphantly on the theme to which the words 'Wer ein holdes Weib errungen' are set. *St. Paul* was given again at the Pauluskirche on 16th March, after which Felix went to Frankfort and was married at the Walloon French Reformed Church on 28th March, to the accompaniment of a wedding chorus for women's voices especially composed as a surprise by Hiller. The couple then went for their honeymoon to Freiburg; the setting of Psalm XLII and the string Quartet in E minor were written at this time; also a pleasant little *Allegretto* composed specially for Cécile, which was never published, but is reproduced in Jacques Petitpierre's book *The Romance of the Mendelssohns*. After this they returned to Frankfort for the summer.

Meanwhile it had been decided that *St. Paul* should be given at the Birmingham Festival of 1837; also the piano Concerto in D minor, which had been composed specially for that purpose in the summer. He therefore had to leave Germany on 24th August to supervise the preliminary arrangements, which meant a most unwelcome break in his holiday.

Here I sit—in the fog—very cross—without my wife—writing to you because your letter of the day before yesterday requires it; otherwise I should hardly do so, for I am much too cross and melancholy to-day. It is nine days since I parted from Cécile at Düsseldorf, the first few were quite bearable, though very wearisome, but now I have got into the whirl of London—great distances—too many people—my head crammed with business and accounts and money matters and arrangements—and it is becoming unbearable, and I wish I were sitting with Cécile and had let Birmingham be Birmingham, and could enjoy life more than I do to-day.

This he wrote to Hiller in a mood of extreme irritation, but he soon found distractions. He played the organ with great success, especially at St. Paul's, where, after the service, the rapt congregation could only be dispersed by the desperate expedient of removing the organ-blower. He had already begun to entertain the idea of an oratorio on the subject of Elijah, and he had some consultations with Klingemann on the subject. On 12th September *St. Paul* was given by the Sacred Harmonic Society, and on the following day Felix left for Birmingham.

The Festival was, as might have been expected, a great personal triumph for him, as composer, pianist and conductor. He played Bach's 'St. Anne' Prelude and Fugue on the organ and performed a few movements from the St. Matthew Passion. The enthusiasm of the inhabitants of Birmingham for his music naturally gratified him, but in letters to his mother and to Hiller he comments indignantly on their complete change of attitude towards Neukomm, who during the last three years had been held in the highest esteem there and was referred to as 'The King of Brummagen':

You will say that his music is not worth anything, and in that no doubt we agree; but still, those who were enraptured then, and now affect such superiority, do not know that. I am indignant about the whole affair, and Neukomm's quiet, equable behaviour appeared to me doubly praiseworthy and dignified compared to theirs.

After the festival he returned to London, was presented with a silver snuff-box by the Sacred Harmonic Society and went through Frankfort to Leipzig, arriving in time for the first concert of the season on 1st October.

Family Meeting

At this time Cécile had not yet made the acquaintance of her husband's family. Journeys from Leipzig to Berlin were at that time no light undertaking, but the sisters, especially Fanny, at first felt some resentment that their new sister-in-law had not been brought to see them. A letter written by Fanny to Cécile before they had met contains even a hint of jealousy:

When I see Felix's works for the first time in print, I look at them with the eyes of a stranger, i.e. criticize them without partiality; but it always makes me sadly recall the time when I used to know his music from its birth. It is so different now, and what a pity it is that fate should have decreed that we are to live so far apart, and that he should have had a wife these eight months whom I have never seen. I tell you candidly that by this time when anybody talks to me about your beauty and your eyes, it makes me quite cross. I have had enough of hearsay and beautiful eyes were not made to be heard.

Shortly after this she came to Leipzig with some friends, and the meeting between her and Cécile gave great satisfaction to both parties. Fanny wrote a thoroughly friendly and sensible description of her to Klingemann:

At last I know my sister-in-law, and I feel as if a load were off my mind, for I cannot deny that I was very uncomfortable and out of sorts at never having seen her. She is amiable, childlike, fresh, bright and even-tempered, and I consider Felix most fortunate for, though inexpressibly fond of him, she does not spoil him, but when he is capricious, treats him with an equanimity which will in course of time most probably cure his fits of irritability altogether. Her presence produces the effect of a fresh breeze, so bright and natural is she.

These words suggest that Cécile, at least at that time, had more vivacity than she is usually credited with. But most descriptions lay more stress on her reserve and elusiveness. Her mother, writing after Felix's death to Paul Mendelssohn, said: 'Cécile's nature has from childhood been gentle, but a little secretive. One has always had to guess at more than she actually expressed.' But Fanny's emphasis on the contrast of temperament between

Felix and Cécile bears out the suggestion that he was far happier with her than he could have been with a wife of more dynamic character. More would be known about their married life if the correspondence between them had been preserved; as it is, the references to her in Felix's published letters, earlier and later, are always charming and affectionate.

CHAPTER V

1838-1844

THE next few years were spent for the most part at Leipzig and involved much musical activity. The concerts flourished; there was an enterprising historical series, including works by composers as unfamiliar as Naumann, Righini and Vogler; there were performances of Beethoven's little-known cantata *Der glorreiche Augenblick* and of Felix's own setting of Psalm XLII. Much music was written in 1838, including the cello Sonata in B flat, Op. 45, the string Quartets in E flat and D from Op. 44 and the setting of Psalm XCV. On 7th February 1838 his first son, Karl Wolfgang Paul, was born; Cécile was seriously ill and caused Felix acute anxiety. In June he conducted the Lower Rhine Festival at Cologne, and the rest of the summer was spent very happily in Berlin. This was Cécile's first meeting with the rest of the family. She was a keen oil painter, and Fanny aptly described her marriage with Felix as the double counterpoint of her own with Wilhelm Hensel. At this time Hensel himself was in England; his picture 'Miriam' had been bought by Queen Victoria just before the coronation, of which he wrote a vivid and entertaining description. In September an epidemic of measles broke out in Berlin, and Felix and his family left hastily for Leipzig in the hope of avoiding it; Felix however caught it on his arrival home, and was prevented from conducting a performance of *St. Paul*, his place being taken by David. The year 1839 was less eventful; the chief compositions were the music to Victor Hugo's *Ruy Blas*, a play that he cordially disliked, the Trio in D minor, the fine setting of Psalm CXIV, and some organ fugues, one of which afterwards became a movement of the second Sonata. He conducted the Lower Rhine Festival at Düsseldorf; shortly after this there was a pleasant visit to Frankfort, where Felix's unaccompanied partsongs were sung out of doors with great success. Earlier in the year Schubert's C major Symphony, which Schumann had brought from Vienna, had its first performance at Leipzig; in September Felix conducted *St. Paul* at Brunswick, and on 12th October his second child, Marie, was born. His mother and his brother Paul came for the christening, and shortly afterwards Hiller, who had just lost his mother, came for a long visit. At one stage Felix decreed that he and Hiller should compose together at the same table. So long as they confined themselves to writing simple partsongs this was very successful, but when they proceeded to works on a larger scale it only brought embarrassment to both composers and was eventually stopped by mutual consent.

The new concert season began in the autumn and included several performances of Schubert's C major Symphony, a programme including all four *Leonora-Fidelio* overtures, and the first performances of the D minor Trio and the 114th Psalm. In March 1840 Liszt came to Leipzig; his virtuosity was admired, but the people of Leipzig were not attracted by his demeanour or by the unceasing wave of publicity that he seemed to carry with him wherever he went. Hiller's oratorio *The Destruction of Jerusalem*, at which he had been working when staying with the Mendelssohns, had its first performance on 2nd April. In June there was a festival in honour of the German printer Gutenberg, and for this Felix composed the *Festgesang*, containing the tune afterwards adapted in England to the hymn *Hark! the herald-angels sing*, and also the *Hymn of Praise*; this soon became enormously popular, though the greater part of it seems now to be rather faded. Almost immediately after the Gutenberg Festival Felix went with Cécile to Schwerin, to conduct *St. Paul* and some other works at a festival. After all this concentrated activity, he would have welcomed a rest, but he had been engaged to conduct the *Hymn of Praise* at the Birmingham Festival in September, and therefore,

42

after a few days in Berlin, he set out for London for the sixth time. After visiting his friends there, including Klingemann, the Moscheles and the Horsleys, he went down to Birmingham. There he conducted the *Hymn of Praise* and selections from Handel's *Jephtha*, after which he extemporized on the organ, combining contrapuntally the two main themes from the chorus that he had just been conducting. He also played the solo part of his piano Concerto in G minor. He then returned to London, gave two organ recitals and returned to Leipzig with the Moscheles and the English critic H. F. Chorley, whom he had met at Brunswick during the previous year. The new Leipzig concert season had begun already, and the *Hymn of Praise* was given at an extra concert at the command of the King of Saxony. For this performance Felix made some alterations and additions, the latter including the scene with the watchman which is by far the most imaginative part of the work.

At this point it is worth looking back for a moment at Mendelssohn's career. There had been troubles and setbacks, such as the early disappointment over *The Wedding of Camacho* and the unfortunate termination of his Düsseldorf appointment. But on the whole it had been remarkably successful, culminating in the Leipzig years. These had been exhausting, but very rewarding; he always felt at home there and in congenial surroundings. Towards Berlin his feelings had always been mixed. As the home of his family he had always been attracted to it, but, so far as his own personal ambitions were concerned, it had usually brought disappointment; even the success with the St. Matthew Passion had caused jealousies among the Berlin musicians. During the remaining years of his life it was to play an important and disturbing part in his affairs.

Frederick William IV, who had just succeeded to the throne of Prussia, was anxious to found a new Academy of Arts in Berlin; there were to be departments for painting, sculpture, architecture and music, and Mendelssohn was offered the post of director of the musical side. The proposal was conveyed to him by von Massov, the Secretary of State, towards the end of 1840. Naturally there was much in it that was tempting; it would bring him near his family, the salary, 3,000 thaler a year, was higher than any that he had earned previously, and the compliment in itself was gratifying. But from the first he felt uncertain about the project; he was anxious to get as much detailed information as possible about his exact duties, and this led to a large amount of tedious and inconclusive correspondence with various officials. In May 1841 he moved from Leipzig to Berlin, and in itself the proximity to his family was most welcome. But for a long time things dragged on in a vague and frustrating manner; having been worked almost to death during the recent Leipzig season, he now felt almost equally exhausted through uncertainty and irritation. This can be felt clearly in the letters of this time; in July he wrote to Klingemann: 'Believe me, Berlin is at the present day the city which is least efficacious, and Leipzig the most beneficial to the public.' And when writing to David at Leipzig a few months later he expressed profound scepticism about the whole arrangement:

You wish to hear some news about the Berlin Conservatory—so do I —but there is none. The affair is on an extensive scale, if it be actually on any scale at all and not merely in the air. The king seems to have a plan for reorganizing the Academy of Arts; this will not be easily effected without entirely changing its present form into a very different one, which they cannot make up their mind to do; there is little use in my advising it, as I do not expect much profit for music from the Academy, either in its present or future form. . . . You will ask, then, what in the world do they want with me just now in Berlin? My answer is, on the one side, I really do not know; on the other, I believe that it is intended to give, during the winter, some great concerts, with the addition of all their best means, and that I am to direct them, some in church and some in the concert-hall, but whether they will ever take place seems to me very doubtful; at all events these are, in my opinion, the only projects which can or will be carried out at this time.

44

In addition to this uncertainty, he also felt that the standard of musical performance in Berlin was far lower than that which he had established at Leipzig, and Devrient's account makes it very clear that this was certainly the case. The prevailing influence at the opera was that of Spontini, of which Devrient writes:

It was altogether a period of false splendour, ruinous to the spirit of German music, of which Spontini had not an idea. The violent contrasts in which he sought his effects, the startling shocks of his *sforzati*, in fact all his effects, calculated to tell only on the nerves and senses of the listeners, could not but demoralize his orchestra.

Making allowance for the instinctive censoriousness of the Teuton towards the Latin, there was undoubtedly some truth in these strictures, and Spontini's essentially showmanlike approach would have been poles apart from that of the more fastidious Mendelssohn.

For some time things moved with maddening slowness and dilatoriness. Mendelssohn drew up a scheme for the musical department, but it produced no immediate result. Despite this irritation he was able to do some composition; the three sets of Variations for piano date from this period. Later in the year he wrote the music for Sophocles' *Antigone* in response to a project of the king for staging Greek tragedies: it was performed for the first time at the king's private theatre at Potsdam. In view of the vagueness of the Berlin appointment he had not formally resigned from his position at Leipzig, though the conducting there was done now by David. Mendelssohn, however, paid a short visit there, playing Beethoven's piano Concerto in C major. In 1842 a new series of concerts was begun in Berlin by order of the king, *St. Paul* being performed at the first. But Mendelssohn found the orchestra difficult and unresponsive, and he had none of the spontaneous support and affection to which he had been accustomed at Leipzig. *Antigone* was successfully given in April at the Berlin Schauspielhaus, and the 'Scottish' Symphony had at last been completed in January. One of his chief sources of pleasure was the series of Sunday morning musical gatherings which had for many years been a regular institution in his family life. These were a pleasant link with his childhood; beginning in a small and intimate way, they had been continued and developed by Fanny, and many distinguished performers took part in them. For Felix they provided a most welcome relief from the far less friendly and cordial atmosphere of his public duties. He went to Leipzig in March for the first performance of the 'Scottish' Symphony, and conducted the Lower Rhine Festival at Düsseldorf in May; shortly after this he went with Cécile to England for a performance of the same Symphony by the Philharmonic Society. This was a great success; a later concert in the same season included the *Hebrides* overture and the D minor Concerto, and, last but not least, the Society wound up the season by giving a fish dinner in Felix's special honour. He played the organ at Christ Church, Newgate Street, and again at Exeter Hall. They visited some cousins at Manchester and when in London stayed with Cécile's relations, the Beneckes, who lived at Denmark Hill; the familiar Song without Words known as the *Spring Song* for piano was written there, and also the six *Christmas Pieces* and the sombre and pathetic piece that was published posthumously as Op. 102, No. 1. Socially the climax of this stay in England was the visit to Buckingham Palace, of which Felix wrote a charming account to his mother. Of course there was music; Mr. Mendelssohn was led to the organ and played 'How lovely are the Messengers' from *St. Paul* with Prince Albert manipulating the stops. Then the queen sang; she produced Felix's first set of songs and, as luck would have it, chose to sing *Italien*, which was not his own composition but one of the songs by Fanny that he had included in the set.

Then I was obliged to confess that Fanny had written the song, which was very hard, but pride must have a fall, and to beg her to sing one of my own also. If I would give her plenty of help she would gladly try, she said, and then she sang the *Pilgerspruch*, 'Las dich nur,' really quite faultlessly, and with charming feeling and expression.

Then the prince consort sang the *Erntelied* from the same set, and finally Felix improvised with great success, introducing themes from most of the pieces of music that had just been per-formed. Later he obtained permission to dedicate the 'Scottish' Symphony to the queen.

In July Felix and Cécile left London; after a short stay at Frankfort they went on a tour to Switzerland, accompanied by Paul Mendelssohn and his wife. Felix enjoyed this thoroughly, and he wrote very happily to his mother from Interlaken, re-minding her of the tour that the family had made through the same country twenty years before. This was followed by another stay at Frankfort, during which he arranged with the publisher Simrock to accept some of Hiller's compositions, a generous and thoughtful act of which Hiller himself remained in complete ignorance until Felix's letter to Simrock was published twenty years later. He then went to Leipzig, conducting a concert at the Gewandhaus, and on to Berlin.

The position there was still vague and unsatisfactory, and at last Felix decided that he could bear it no longer and made arrangements for an audience with the king, at which he pro-posed to send in his resignation. When this was told to the family, however, his mother was terribly upset; eventually, at the interview with the king, the situation was clarified considerably. There were to be fixed bodies of singers and players to perform under Felix's direction; until these were formed, he could be free to travel and live where he liked, so long as he was prepared to come to Berlin whenever the king needed him. His salary was to be 1500 thaler a year. After some deliberation he agreed to these terms, and throughout the interview the king seems to have handled him with great skill and tact. His personal relations with Felix were always friendly, and during the previous summer he had given him the Ordre pour le Mérite.

This last arrangement naturally caused great delight to the Mendelssohns in Berlin and left Felix with at least a more definite idea of what was expected of him. In the spring of 1842 he had been appointed *Kapellmeister* to the King of Saxony; from this he now had to resign, but instead he received permission to found a Conservatory at Leipzig, a project that appealed to him greatly. And the King of Prussia commissioned him to write music for *A Midsummer Night's Dream*, *The Tempest*, Racine's *Athalie* and Sophocles' *Oedipus at Colonus*. He was also hard at work on a revised version of *Die erste Walpurgisnacht*, originally written eleven years earlier. He returned to Leipzig in the autumn and was soon happily occupied and finding the atmosphere far more congenial than that of Berlin. It had been arranged that he should go to Berlin on 17th December to conclude the final negotiations about his position there; eventually, however, he had to go sooner owing to the sudden death of his mother on the 12th, which seems to have been as swift and painless as that of her husband seven years before. This naturally was a very deep sorrow to Felix, though less overwhelming than the loss of his father; he had now more definite work to distract him, and the comfort of his wife and children, of whom the third, Paul, had been born on 18th January 1841. He now became owner of the family house in Berlin, but he soon had to return to his many duties at Leipzig.

By January 1843 he drew up the plans for the Conservatory. He and Schumann were to be in charge of composition and piano, Moritz Hauptmann was to teach harmony and counter-point, David violin and orchestral playing, Carl Ferdinand Becker the organ and Christian August Pohlenz singing; un-fortunately the last of these died before the opening of the school. The revised *Erste Walpurgisnacht* was performed with great success in February; a few days later there was a concert devoted to music by Berlioz, including the *King Lear* overture. Berlioz's visit is thus described in Fanny's diary:

Berlioz was at Leipzig at the time with us, and his odd behaviour gave so much offence that Felix was continually being called upon to smooth somebody's ruffled feathers. When the time for parting came Berlioz offered to exchange batons, 'as the ancient warriors exchanged their armour,' and in return for Felix's pretty light stick of whalebone covered with white leather sent an enormous cudgel of lime-tree with the bark on, and an open letter, beginning 'Le mien est grossier, le tien est simple.' A friend of Berlioz who brought the two translated this sentence, 'I am coarse and you are simple' and was in great perplexity how to conceal the apparent rudeness from Felix.

As contrast to this rather prim and censorious description, it is worth quoting in full Berlioz's exuberant letter:

Great chief! We have promised to exchange tomahawks! Here is mine, it is coarse, yours is simple. Only squaws and pale-faces like ornate weapons. Be my brother, and when the Great Spirit has sent us to hunt in the Land of Souls, may our warriors hang up our tomahawks together on the door of the Council Chamber.

It is not known how Felix reacted to this Fenimore Cooper-esque outburst, but his congenital dislike for Berlioz's music did not prevent the two men from remaining on thoroughly friendly terms. About this time Niels Gade's first symphony, in C minor, was performed at Leipzig; Felix took a great fancy to it and wrote him a most friendly and encouraging letter.

On 9th March came the celebration of the centenary of the Gewandhaus concerts, the programme being chosen from the works of former cantors. Another concert, consisting entirely of music by Bach, was the occasion of the unveiling of the monu-ment to Bach, a project that had been started in 1840. During this spring Joachim, at the age of twelve, came to Leipzig, and he and Felix became close friends. The Mendelssohns' fourth child, Felix, was born on 4th May, and, apart from a journey to Dresden to conduct *St. Paul*, Mendelssohn remained at Leipzig throughout the summer. He and Wagner both contributed a composition for the unveiling of a statue of Frederick Augustus I of Saxony at Dresden. They were settings of the same poem, specially written for the occasion, Wagner's being for men's voices unaccompanied and Mendelssohn's for men's voices and brass. We have it on Wagner's authority that his own 'simple and heartfelt composition entirely eclipsed the complex artificialities of Mendelssohn.' Felix's composition was printed many years later in the *Musical Times* for June 1906; there is nothing particularly complex about it except for the ingenuity with which *God save the King*, which was also the Saxon national anthem, is worked into the harmonic texture. Much music of greater importance was composed at this time, including the music for *A Midsummer Night's Dream* (apart from the much earlier overture) and for *Athalie*, and the cello Sonata in D. On the whole this was a remarkably happy and productive period, spoilt only by some verbose and irritating correspondence about his Berlin position, which cast a depressing shadow over the picture.

Antigone, *A Midsummer Night's Dream* and *Athalie* were to be performed in Berlin in September 1843; the music however was not ready and the performances were postponed. *Antigone* was eventually given on 19th September at Potsdam and *A Midsummer Night's Dream* at the same place on 18th October and several times subsequently at Berlin. On every occasion the music was enthusiastically praised, but the play was often severely criticized. In 1831 Felix had been warned by some worthy Italian citizens against reading a comedy by Shakespeare called *Il sonno d'una notte di mezza state*, in which 'the stale device occurred of a piece rehearsed in the play, and it was full of anachronisms and childish ideas.' Now many equally worthy citizens of Berlin made similarly inept comments, one thinking that it was by Tieck, not Shakespeare, another suggesting that it had been translated by Shakespeare from German into English, and the general opinion being that the scenes with the clowns were vulgar, that it was extraordinary that so exalted a personage as the king could have approved of it and lamentable that music as lovely as Felix's should have been wasted on so inferior a play. All this shows how German and Italian alike could be puzzled by the peculiar blend of poetry and humour so characteristic of *A Midsummer Night's Dream*. The Mendelssohn family, how-ever, could appreciate it; as Fanny sagely remarked: 'They were really brought up on the *Midsummer Night's Dream* and Felix especially had made it their own.' After these performances Felix returned to Leipzig, where Gade's symphony was per-formed again and Macfarren's *Chevy Chase* overture was given. Shortly after this Felix wrote a letter to Macfarren, towards the end of which he said: 'God bless you, my dear Sir; excuse these hasty lines; they pack up all my things, and I am in a black, or at least a greyish mood.' These words, written incidentally in English, suggest vividly Felix's reactions to the prospect of leaving Leipzig for Berlin.

Before his departure he had realized that he would be in Berlin for some time, and therefore it was arranged that Hiller should conduct the concerts at the Gewandhaus for this season. He was in Berlin from the end of November to the end of February, and on the whole the winter of 1843–4 was happier than might have been expected. His relations with the Berlin orchestra seem to have been more cordial than formerly, and there was plenty of music to distract his mind from official worries and irritations. Christmas festivities, which had been in abeyance last year owing to the death of his mother, were now held lavishly in the family house. At this time he did his best to help his friend Sterndale Bennett to get the Professorship of Music at Edinburgh University; it was, however, eventually given to Hugo Henry Pierson.

The compositions of this period were mainly ecclesiastical; in March 1844 he conducted performances of Handel's *Israel in Egypt* and Beethoven's ninth Symphony. These involved a great deal of energy and nervous strain, leaving him eventually in a state of extreme exhaustion. The King of Prussia was anxious for him to compose music for Aeschylus' *Eumenides*; a casual remark of his on the difficulty of the undertaking was interpreted as a refusal, and some pompous and long-winded correspondence followed, causing him considerable irritation. It was with great relief that he was able to return with his family to Frankfort immediately after Easter.

CHAPTER VI

1845–1847

MEANWHILE he had been approached by the Philharmonic Society in London, who were eager to engage him as conductor for the 1844–5 season. This he accepted gladly, making it clear that he could not come till after Easter, and he arrived in London early in May, staying with Klingemann. He had intended to perform Schubert's C major Symphony, but the orchestra refused to take it seriously, and in the finale their behaviour became so uproarious that Mendelssohn indignantly withdrew the work and, along with it, his own *Ruy Blas* overture. This, however, was the only blot on an otherwise brilliant and successful season. The whole of the *Midsummer Night's Dream* music was given, and it was received with great enthusiasm; other high lights were Joachim's performance of Beethoven's violin Concerto and Mendelssohn's own of the fourth piano Concerto, in G, which had always been a particular favourite of his and was at that time hardly known in England. Sterndale Bennett played his own C minor Concerto. In addition to the Philharmonic concerts there was much music-making, private and public, and the usual endless round of social engagements, including a visit to relations at Manchester. He played his cello Sonata in D with Piatti, for whom he intended to write a concerto, and he was working hard at an edition of *Israel in Egypt* for the Handel Society.

He arrived at Frankfort, exhausted but happy, in July, and in a letter of thanks to Klingemann wrote:

I found my family well, and we had a joyful meeting when I arrived here on Saturday, in health and happiness after a very rapid journey. Cécile looks so well again, tanned by the sun but without the least trace of her former indisposition; my first glance told this when I came into the room, but to this day I cannot cease rejoicing afresh every time I look at her. The children are as brown as Moors and play all day long in the garden.

Not only Cécile but also the children had been ill during his absence, though the latter fact had been kept from him. Now they had recovered, were developing rapidly and had become a constant source of delight to their father; his letters describe many pleasant family incidents such as the horrifying moment when Cécile came in and found him teaching the wrong fingering of the scale of C major to his daughter Marie. The 1844–5 season of concerts at the Gewandhaus at Leipzig was conducted by Gade. At the end of September Mendelssohn left Frankfort for Berlin. His time with his family had been delightful, and it had not been idle, as he had conducted the Bavarian Palatinate Festival at Zweibrücken in July and in September he finished his violin Concerto, ideas for which had been in his head for six years. As usual he felt acutely depressed by his return to Berlin, and indeed his dislike for it had become almost an obsession. His immediate object was to obtain release from all official duties, only undertaking any occasional commissions required by the king. This was granted, his salary now being reduced to 1000 thaler a year. He stayed in Berlin till the end of November, however, as the king desired a performance of *St. Paul* at the Singakademie; after the final rehearsal of this his friends gave a party in his honour. During this stay at Berlin his portrait was painted by Hensel. The termination of his appointment there caused great distress to Fanny, but in view of his deteriorating health and the friction that seemed to accompany all his dealings with the officials it was the only possible course.

Meanwhile during his absence his youngest son, Felix, had had an alarmingly severe attack of measles, from which he took long to recover; about the same time Rebecka Dirichlet and her husband, who were in Rome, were seriously ill. Mendelssohn

Felix Mendelsohn Bartholdy

THE OLD BUILDING OF THE LEIPZIG CONSERVATORIUM

MONUMENT TO MENDELSSOHN AT LEIPZIG
Destroyed in 1936

FACSIMILE OF A LETTER FROM MENDELSSOHN

Felix Mendelssohn Bartholdy

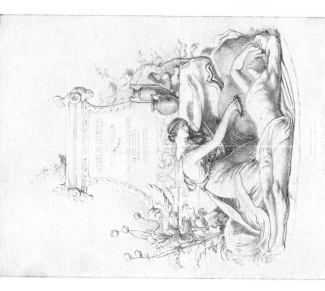

LITHOGRAPHIC TITLE-PAGES TO MUSIC PRINTED IN THE MIDDLE OF THE NINETEENTH CENTURY

Left: Piano score of the oratorio *Elias* by Mendelssohn, Op. 70. Bonn, N. Simrock. Drawing by Julius Hübner, 1847, lithograph print by C. Hahn. *Right*: Music to Sophocles' *Antigone* by Felix Mendelssohn-Bartholdy, Op. 55. Leipzig, F. Kistner. Drawing by Julius Hübner, 1842.

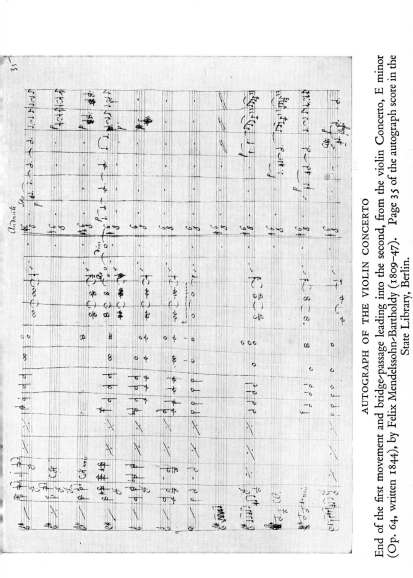

AUTOGRAPH OF THE VIOLIN CONCERTO

End of the first movement and bridge-passage leading into the second, from the violin Concerto, E minor (Op. 64, written 1844), by Felix Mendelssohn-Bartholdy (1809–47). Page 35 of the autograph score in the State Library, Berlin.

FASCIMILE OF A PAGE OF 'ELIJAH' (MANUSCRIPT VOCAL SCORE)

remained at Frankfort for the greater part of 1845, with much composition to occupy him. The music for *Athalie* and for *Oedipus at Colonus* was finished; there was a tentative suggestion from the King of Prussia that he should write music for the whole of Aeschylus' *Oresteia* trilogy, but on his replying that no living composer was competent to deal adequately with it, the matter was allowed quietly to die. *Elijah*, which was to be performed at Birmingham the following year, was now steadily taking shape, and he already had ideas for the unfinished *Christus*. The string Quintet in B flat and the Trio in C minor also date from 1845. Earlier in the year *Antigone* had been performed in London, at Covent Garden, and Mendelssohn was much amused by a picture of the chorus, very much in the style of George Cruikshank, that appeared in *Punch*.[1] In June he was asked by the King of Saxony to take up once more his post at Leipzig; as the result of this, he had settled by September in a town for which he had always had a particularly warm affection, and in the house that proved to be his last home. At his first concert, at which Clara Schumann played, he was greeted with a spontaneous enthusiasm that must have gladdened his heart. Charlotte Dolby (later Madame Sainton-Dolby) and Jenny Lind appeared at later concerts in the same season. In September his fifth and last child, Lilli, was born. But his health was not good, and he was becoming increasingly prone to fits of weariness and gloom. In December he wrote to say that, though he had decided to go to Birmingham, he could only undertake to conduct his own works there.

On the other hand his work at the Leipzig Conservatory was carried on with the greatest energy; Grove has given a most vivid description of his composition classes, based on information from former pupils. He was keen and stimulating, but highly fastidious; it is not surprising to hear of him saying, in English, to

[1] Reproduced in Grove's *Dictionary of Music and Musicians*, vol. ii, article 'Caricature.'

an English pupil: 'very ungentlemanlike modulation.' His temper could be explosive, but both pupils and teachers can take comfort from an incident in which he was beaten by a contrapuntal problem. 'You can't tell where to place the next note?' —'No'—'I am glad of that, for neither can I.' Moscheles was at that time professor of the piano at the Conservatory. Meanwhile *Oedipus at Colonus* and *Athalie* had both been performed in Berlin. Early in 1846 he was commissioned to compose a *Lauda Sion* for a festival at Liége; it was eventually given there on 11th June, the performance, which was far from adequate, being followed by exuberant festivities. He conducted the Lower Rhine Festival at Aachen in May and June, with Jenny Lind singing in *The Creation* and *Alexander's Feast*. From there he went to Düsseldorf, where he was twice serenaded, owing to the incompatibility of the two rival 'Liedertafeln.' This must have recalled vividly the quarrelsome atmosphere of Düsseldorf from which he had suffered previously, and he was particularly sorry to find that his friend Julius Rietz was being treated so badly there that he had decided to leave. All these functions were exhausting him more and more, however enjoyable many of them were at the time, and he was at the same time working hard at *Elijah*, which, apart from the actual composition of the music, involved him in correspondence of all kinds. At one moment he would be writing to Schubring about some problem connected with the libretto ('May Elisha sing soprano? or is this inadmissible, as in the same chapter he is described as a baldhead?'), at another to Moscheles protesting against the proposed exclusion from the Philharmonic Orchestra of a few players who had spoken disrespectfully to him last time he had been in London.

At length he arrived in London on 17th August, and the performance took place on the 26th. The chief soloists were Maria CaradoriAllen, Maria Hawes, Charles Lockey and Staudigl. The success was overwhelming; writing to his brother

Paul, Mendelssohn said he had never heard so successful a first performance of any work of his: 'It was quite evident at the first rehearsal in London that they liked it, and liked to sing and play it; but I own I was far from anticipating that it would acquire such fresh vigour and impetus at the performance.' When it was first performed in London, the Prince Consort sent to Mendelssohn the book of words that he had used, inscribed with these words:

To the noble artist who, though encompassed by the Baal-worship of false art, by his genius and study has succeeded, like another Elijah, in faithfully preserving the worship of true art; once more habituating the ear, amid the giddy whirl of empty frivolous sound, to the pure tones of sympathetic feeling and legitimate harmony; to the great master who, by the tranquil current of his thoughts, reveals to us the gentle whisperings, as well as the mighty strife of the elements, to him is this written in grateful remembrance by   ALBERT.

After the Birmingham Festival he returned to London with the Moscheles, stayed for four days at Ramsgate with the Beneckes, and crossed the Channel on 6th October. Eventually he arrived at Leipzig, very tired and worn out; this is very clearly felt in a letter written to Fanny about this time:

I cannot make up my mind to undertake a journey or anything else, but after the exertions of this summer, and all the travelling I have had to go through, I am now leading a vegetable existence. Ever since my arrival, when a single glance told me that all were well and happy, I have done nothing but eat, sleep and take walks, and yet I never seem to get enough of either occupation.

He was preparing Elijah for the press and with his usual scrupulousness was perpetually thinking of possible alterations and improvements. He was still concerned with possible opera libretti and started work on Loreley to a text by Geibel. He also began writing the oratorio Christus, which had been in his mind for some time. He was much distressed by the illness and death of his servant Johann Krebs, who was a great favourite with all the family. Despite his weariness he was busy making arrange, ments for the Conservatory. On 3rd February 1847 his birthday was celebrated at the Moscheles'; there were some cheerful amateur theatricals, Joachim and the Moscheles acting a charade on the word 'Gewandhaus.'

At this stage his spirits and enjoyment of life seem to have revived considerably, but soon his travels had to start again. After a performance of *St. Paul* at Leipzig he was engaged to go to London to conduct the revised version of *Elijah* three times with the Sacred Harmonic Society. He travelled to England with Joachim and stayed with the Klingemanns. The three performances took place at the Exeter Hall and were followed by a fourth. One of these was attended by the queen and the prince consort, who wrote on his book of words the note already quoted. The first performance was unsatisfactory and severely criticized in the *Athenaeum*. In addition to the four London performances there was one at Manchester and another at Birming, ham, all six coming within a fortnight. There were many other functions, musical and otherwise, including a visit to Buckingham Palace. It all amounted to far more than was good for anyone in Mendelssohn's state of health; it was remarked that he looked ill and aged, and, when pressed to prolong his visit, he said, sadly: 'Ah! I wish I may not already have stayed too long here. One more week of this unremitting fatigue, and I should be killed outright.'

He crossed the Channel on 9th May; at Herbesthal there was a highly irritating delay, owing to a police official mistaking him for a Dr. Mendelssohn who was suspect politically. Eventually he arrived at Frankfort, and in a few days' time came the news of the sudden death of Fanny Hensel: when conducting her choir, she was seized by a paralytic stroke from which she never recovered. For Felix this was a terrible shock; the news was broken too abruptly, and he fell to the ground in a state of unconsciousness from which it took him some time to return. Soon the family went to Baden-Baden, where Wilhelm Hensel and Paul Mendelssohn joined them; they then went on to Switzerland, staying mostly at Interlaken. Felix did a number of water-colour sketches but it was some time before he could bring himself to do any composition. Eventually, at Interlaken, he wrote the restless and passionate string Quartet in F minor, Op. 80. After this came the two central movements of an unfinished Quartet, and various smaller works, including one of his finest songs, the *Nachtlied*. Commissions of all kinds began to flood him; the Philharmonic Society wanted a symphony for 1848, *Elijah* was to be performed in Berlin and Vienna, but he could feel no lasting hope that any of them would be carried out. H. F. Chorley has left an interesting account of his last meeting with Mendelssohn in Switzerland; Felix talked about Rossini's *William Tell* and Donizetti's *The Daughter of the Regiment* in a manner that suggested a mellower and more tolerant attitude towards Italian music; he inquired with interest about Verdi.

My very last memory is the sight of him turning down the road, to wind back to Interlaken alone; while we turned up to cross the Wengernalp to Grindelwald. I thought even then, as I followed his figure, looking none the younger for the loose dark coat and the wide-brimmed straw hat bound with black crape, which he wore, that he was too much depressed and worn, and walked too heavily. But who could have dreamed that his days on earth were so rapidly drawing to a close?

They returned to Leipzig in September; the visit to Switzerland had undoubtedly done him some good, but much of this was undone when he went to Berlin and saw Fanny's rooms, left as they had been when she died. There were times when he seemed more cheerful; on 9th September he went to see his friend Livia Frege, with whom he went through his recent songs, but he was there seized by a shivering fit, and on his return home he went to bed. Soon he seemed to be recovering, and on the 25th he wrote to Paul: 'God be praised, I am now daily getting better, and my strength is returning more and more.' And in the same letter: 'I believe you would do me more good than all my bitter medicine. Write me a couple of lines soon again, and be sure you agree to come.' On 28th October he seemed so much better that he went out with Cécile, but soon he was much worse again, and on the 30th Paul was sent for. Eventually he died on 4th November. [1] The funeral rites began on 7th November, the coffin being followed by a long procession as it was carried to the Paulinerkirche, accompanied by an arrangement by Moscheles of the fine Song without Words in E minor from Book V. In church the choir sang the chorale 'To Thee, O Lord,' the chorus 'Happy and blest' from *St. Paul*, and after the funeral oration the final chorus from Bach's St. Matthew Passion. The procession then proceeded to Berlin, and there, early in the morning, to the accompaniment of 'Jesu, meine Freude,' the body was laid in the family vault next to that of his much-loved sister.

Cécile survived him for barely six years, dying of consumption in September 1853; Rebecka Dirichlet died of apoplexy in 1858 as suddenly as her sister Fanny. Paul lived till 1874, far longer than the others, having been a most devoted guardian to his nephews and nieces. Of Felix's two daughters the elder, Marie, married Victor Benecke, and their son became a Fellow of Magdalen College, Oxford. Lili married Adolph Wach; a very sympathetic picture of her is to be found in Ethel Smyth's *Impressions that Remained*. The eldest son, Karl, became a professor at Heidelberg; the second, Paul, was a very gifted scientist who, like his father, died at the early age of thirty-eight.

[1] Evidence produced by R. Sterndale Bennett in an article that appeared in *Music & Letters*, XLVI, 1955, suggests strongly that Mendelssohn's death was the result of an apoplectic condition started by the sudden shock of his sister's death.

CHAPTER VII

PERSONALITY AND INFLUENCE

'THE epoch for expansion and extended analysis has passed away: the novelties of knotty points and subtle analogies are undesired: we want strong emotion, but it must be concentrated; it must smite, sudden as the electric fluid, it must draw blood. And this is Mendelssohn.'

'That Mendelssohn possessed a natural vein of such rich, flowing melody as Mozart and Beethoven commanded, cannot be claimed for him. Yet as a melodist he has been misunder-stood and undervalued in no common degree—the fate, by the way, of every composer who is more than a mere melodist. Those who have passed hasty judgment on him as "dry" have done so rather on the strength of some one work that does not suit their humour than on the bulk of his writings.'

Of these pronouncements the first was made by H. J. Gauntlett during Mendelssohn's lifetime, when writing about the organ sonatas; the second appeared shortly after his death in H. F. Chorley's *Modern German Music*. The one acclaims him as a passionate romantic, the other defends him as an imperfectly appreciated intellectual, and it would be hard to decide which of the two makes the odder reading at the present day. The work to which Gauntlett devotes this extravagant panegyric is the first movement of the organ Sonata in B flat. He describes this as 'Bach Prelude, but not Bach' and proceeds to call attention to the 'heart-quivering march of the pedal from the lower E flat to the F,' a passage which proves on inspection to be a chromatic progression, effective enough, but mild and respectable when put beside the harmonic splendour of J. S. Bach. And in all

61

probability it was this very fact that endeared the passage to the eminently respectable Dr. Gauntlett; it was rich without being extravagant and edifying without savouring of 'enthusiasm.' And, turning to Chorley's criticism, we can see at once how the love of counterpoint that now seems one of the most attractive features of Mendelssohn's style was to him 'hard and dry'; a sign of musical immaturity that was happily held in check in later years. Despite Dr. Gauntlett's extravagant tone, it is fairly clear that the ideal of both critics was a tempered moderation of mind and emotion that appeared to them to be a consummation more glorious than many more positive and adventurous characteristics.

Something of the same attitude can be found if we turn from contemporary English estimates of his music to those of his character. The Rev. H. R. Haweis, in *Music and Morals*, wrote as follows:

In this age of mercenary musical manufacture and art degradation, Mendelssohn towers above his contemporaries like a great moral light-house in the midst of a dark and troubled sea. His light always shone strong and pure. The winds of heaven were about his head, and the STILL SMALL VOICE was in his heart. In a lying generation he was pure, and not popularity nor gain could tempt him to sully the pages of his spotless inspiration with one meretricious effect or one impure association.

Here again the language is flowery and extravagant, but the main emotion underlying it is the worship of a kind of sanctified respectability. It finds yet more exuberant expression in the novel *Charles Auchester* by Elizabeth Sara Sheppard, of which the hero, Seraphael, an alleged portrayal of Mendelssohn, is a kind of plaster-cast saint, with occasional bursts of a rather embarrassing playfulness.

Against all this may be set the comment of Goethe quoted in an earlier chapter: 'He has the smallest possible modicum of the phlegmatic, and the maximum of the opposite quality.' This at once suggests the restlessness that remained a characteristic of Felix all his life, and was liable, in his music, to result in a rather ineffectual fussiness. The autocratic determination of his father and the anxious intensity of 'Tante Jette' both found echoes in his personality, and it seems doubtful whether these very dissimilar traits were ever completely reconciled to each other. He was certainly, as S. S. Stratton discreetly expressed it, 'never backward in passing judgment'; as a boy he was equally sure of himself, whether he was criticizing the modulations in Herr Boguslavski's Symphony or expressing his enthusiasm for the Swiss scenery or castigating the musical frivolity of the French. His devotion to the later works of Beethoven remained unshaken even by paternal disapproval; on the other hand, in more practical matters, his inability to see the points of view of others when things did not go as he wished often led to unnecessary unpleasantness, as during the disturbing contretemps just before the first performance of *Son and Stranger*.

Outbursts of this kind, rare in his early years, became more frequent during the Düsseldorf period; the increasing tension can be felt even in the glowing panegyric of Elise Polko, who writes with the most gushing hero-worship:

Perhaps, also, the unconcealed endeavours of the fiery young master to secure the first place for his beloved art caused the representative of the 'irritable race of poets' to lose patience; at all events there soon arose greater or lesser points of collision. . . . No decided opinion can be given on the subject of these complicated Düsseldorf conflicts, much less can they be discussed in detail; too many recent graves lie around on every side, on which the grass has not yet grown; who can have the courage to invade these sacred resting-places?

Later in the same chapter this authoress quotes with approval a rebuke administered by Mendelssohn to some friends who had spoken slightingly of the chorus in praise of wine that ends the third portion of Haydn's *Seasons*.

Father Haydn can well forgive your calumny, and can afford to wait patiently till you once more come to your senses. Let the frothy period of youth pass away, and then sing his chorus to a glass of wine, and tell me whether it still seems insipid. At this moment the wine itself is your chief object. When Haydn wrote that chorus, he did not drink wine as you do, merely to enjoy it, but only in order to gain strength for his work, and to rejoice in the strength it imparted. So I say again, wait.

This illustrates well the preaching, moralizing approach to art that found so much more favour in the nineteenth than in the twentieth century. It was particularly characteristic of a period at which the composer tended more and more to regard himself not merely as a skilled craftsman but also as an inspired prophet. It coincided to some extent with the growth of conscious nationalism in music, and Mendelssohn, like many other German composers of the time, liked to regard himself as a champion of Teutonic seriousness and solidity against Latin flimsiness and frivolity. On the other hand this attitude was tempered by his great sociability, and he was unable to resist the charm and liveliness of the French despite his disapproval of their music. His attitude towards Italian music mellowed in his later years, and on one occasion he administered a gentle rebuke to some superior young men who were belittling Donizetti.

It is possible to attach too much significance to this tendency to moralize; now regarded with a sometimes exaggerated horror, it was then thoroughly fashionable, and Mendelssohn, as a boy of exceptional charm and vivacity, may well have been encouraged to air his views in a rather priggish manner. It will be remembered that Goethe was anxious lest the boy's head should be turned by gushing female flattery. In the family circle, on the other hand, there would have been little danger of this; there, any over-dogmatic utterances were greeted with the nickname 'Sir Oracle' and firmly discouraged by Felix's parents, and, perhaps still more so, by his highly critical elder sister. In an earlier chapter attention has been called to the contrast between the wealthy surroundings in which Felix was born and those of his grandfather. Equally marked is that between the luxurious back-ground of Felix's childhood and his extremely thorough and rigorous education, and his parents' reluctance to do anything that might suggest to him that his own gifts were in any way exceptional. In the Mendelssohn family the tradition of hard work was strongly established, and Devrient has described vividly how, when he and Felix were small boys, their conversation would be interrupted by Leah Mendelssohn saying severely: 'Felix, are you doing nothing?' If, as a boy, he sometimes seemed to be too dogmatic and self-assured, this may have owed something to his early social success, but more to a strain of natural intolerance inherited from his father. Much as they appreciated his musical gifts, his parents proceeded with great caution before consenting to his following a musical career. At a time when there is a tendency to view every human activity in the light of its economic background, it is assumed too readily that a comfortable financial situation is bound to lead to self-indulgence; in the case of Mendelssohn this was certainly not the case. Self-indulgence played no part in his life, and if any criticism can be levelled against his family background, it is that it inculcated into him the restlessness and the inability to relax that were more than anything responsible for his early death.

It has already been said that he had in him a streak of extreme sensitiveness that seemed to look back, not so much to his parents, as to his warm-hearted and highly strung Aunt Henriette. Schubring, in an article written for the *Musical World* in 1866, suggests, probably with some truth, that this would have been less excessive if he had been sent to school instead of being educated at home. It took various forms, the most notable being his exceptional vulnerability to criticism of his music. Some-times it asserted itself at unexpected moments, temporarily under-mining his normal self-confidence; a notable instance in his early days was the occasion when, after one of Moscheles's concerts, he was asked to play, but was suddenly overcome by nerves and broke down completely. It occurred a few years later, when he and Devrient were about to broach to the formidable Zelter their project for performing the St. Matthew Passion. 'If he is abusive, I shall go. I cannot squabble with him,' said Felix, to which the more robust Devrient replied: 'He is sure to be abusive, but I will take the squabbling in hand myself.' Conscientious and unsparing of himself in all his work, he was liable to lose patience over irksome and sordid details; this was particularly noticeable in the troubles at Düsseldorf and, later on, during the prolonged irritation and uncertainty that accompanied his official dealings with the King of Prussia. He was always acutely sensitive to his environment, and it was necessary for him to feel that he was surrounded by friends wherever he was. From this point of view he was always particularly happy in London. Leipzig he always found thoroughly congenial; also Frankfort, which had the particularly happy associations of his engagement and marriage. In Paris, for all his enjoyment of French society, he felt isolated; in Düsseldorf he began happily but soon found the atmosphere poisoned by intrigues, from which he could only extract himself by a sudden and drastic withdrawal. Worst of all was Berlin, despite the happy associations of his childhood. Even during his early successes there he was conscious of the jealousy of older musicians, and in his later years the city seemed to have become the embodiment of all that was sinister, and the prospect of every fresh visit to it seemed to fill him with more horror than the last. At no time in his life had he the robust determination that could have enabled him to break through all oppositions, however strenuous.

As a child he was noted for his high spirits and his generous and impulsive affection for his fellow creatures, and for many years these qualities seemed to lose little of their old spontaneity. His good looks and charm of manner and speech impressed everyone with whom he came into contact, and, apart from his music, he had many social accomplishments—dancing, riding, billiards and chess. His water-colour sketches showed considerable talent, and even as a child he was a remarkably vivid letter-writer. With all these gifts it is not surprising that he went into society far more than the average composer of his day. This may well have limited the range of his musical invention; on the other hand there is no reason to suppose that he ever consciously wrote down to the level of his surroundings and, with all his great social success, he seems to have been quite free from personal vanity. In later years he grew more irritable, largely as the result of overwork and constant nervous strain, but it was more often on behalf of others than for purely personal reasons; he was filled with generous indignation by such incidents as the proposed dismissal from the Philharmonic Orchestra of some players who had behaved disrespectfully towards him on a previous occasion, the fickleness of the inhabitants of Birmingham towards Neukomm and an attempt to cause dissension between himself and Spohr in England.

As a conductor he was immensely thorough and had the power to inspire great enthusiasm, though this could be marred by the irritability of a highly strung temperament prone to rely more on nervous impulse than on clearly considered judgments. As a teacher he had the same strength and weakness; he was stimulating and capable of great kindness, but his temper was uncertain and liable to be unreasonably upset by trifles, such as the colour and untidiness of a female student's hair. He was fully aware of these defects, and as early as 1839 he admitted in a letter to Professor Naumann, of Bonn, that he had not the patience necessary for a good teacher.

Enough has already been said about his devotion to his family and, especially, of his deep reverence for his father. They, in their turn, seem to have regarded him as a wayward and lovable child who never completely grew up. His restlessness and incessant social activities were sometimes a worry to them, and his father, in particular, was obviously hoping that in due course 'the boy would settle down and find himself a wife.' In the period of deep family sorrow that followed Abraham Mendelssohn's death it was felt strongly that marriage was the only thing that could rouse Felix from his grief, and at Fanny's advice he went to Frankfort with the deliberate idea of seeking out a wife. This does not seem a particularly romantic or promising prelude to a marriage, and, in view of his usual impulsiveness, it is surprising to see him deliberately leaving Frankfort, to test his feelings for a time, before proposing to Cécile. There can be no doubt that he was deeply in love with her and that the marriage brought him great happiness, but it did not diminish the very strong influence of his own family background, and indeed it may have seemed to him to be a kind of extension of it. The family themselves could not be happy about it until they were satisfied that Cécile was of the kind that could fit happily into their own very individual way of life and, as has already been suggested, Cécile, with her quiet sympathy and gentleness, was able to do this more easily than a woman of more dynamic or self-assertive temperament. It is perhaps significant that, during the sad final months after Fanny's death, Felix had planned to take his wife and children back to Berlin and live in the same house with Paul and Rebecka. As might be expected, he was a most devoted father, and it is most regrettable that he did not live to see his children grow up. And it is important to remember that our knowledge of his married life is severely limited by the fact that his correspondence with Cécile was never published and may well have been destroyed.

It was in his passionate love for his family that Mendelssohn's Jewish blood showed itself most strongly, though it may also claim some credit for his shrewdness, adaptability and mercurial vitality. The extent to which it affected his music is far harder to decide, as Jewish composers differ so greatly from each other. In the music of some, such as Mahler and Bloch, is to be found a feverish and tortured emotion; on the other hand, in the works of Meyerbeer the predominating trait is an unfailing *savoir faire* that knows precisely what it wants and can achieve it without any great emotional struggles. Both chronologically and temperamentally Mendelssohn was more akin to the second of these two types, though he was by far the greatest of them. He lacked Meyerbeer's bouncing energy and showmanship, but he had finer taste and a more individual creative imagination. And though he must be classed with the smoother, less passionate composers, there are here and there signs that he was capable of expressing a more powerful and forthright emotion which hardly ever succeeded in finding full expression.

It was just this last fact that contributed so much to the enormous popularity of his music in England. For those to whom Schumann and Chopin were disturbingly emotional and 'modern,' and Wagner and Brahms unknown quantities, Mendelssohn's conservatism, melodiousness and unfailingly good manners seemed not merely pleasant and decorous, but worthy of the deepest affection. This music made them feel at home, always a particularly endearing trait to the English, its sentiment made a singularly tender appeal and its high spirits were pleasantly exhilarating without descending to vulgar boisterousness. It must also be remembered that, of all the great classical composers, Handel had by far the widest following in England during Mendelssohn's lifetime; native composers were still producing worthy imitations of his idiom, which probably still sounded more contemporary there than in any other European country. Haydn was the most eminent composer after Handel's day who had spent a considerable period of time in England, but at that time he was more distinguished as a writer of instrumental than of vocal music, and had not yet composed his two great oratorios. Mendelssohn, when he visited England, had also made his mark more by instrumental than by vocal music, but his youthful brilliance and charm immediately won innumerable friends for himself and his music, and when in later years he wrote his oratorios, these developed a dearly loved tradition in what seemed to be a new and exciting way. The lack of rhythmic variety that now strikes us immediately on turning from a Handel to a Mendelssohn oratorio would then have met with no adverse criticism; it was the natural thing for composers to write mainly in phrases of four or eight bars, and the revival of interest in the sixteenth century had not yet come to awaken English musicians to the possibilities of a more flexible rhythmic style. And what Tovey describes as 'the parochial softness' of the solos would have made an instantaneous appeal to many who found Beethoven rugged and Mozart coldly elegant.

Outside England Mendelssohn's music was not so widely and uncritically acclaimed, largely because there was greater knowledge of the work of his more adventurous contemporaries, but it is worth recording that two musicians as dissimilar as Berlioz and Schumann held him in the highest regard, and indeed Schumann, in some of his later works, came decidedly under his influence. In England this was, of course, widespread, and usually with deplorable results. S. S. Wesley and Sterndale Bennett had sufficient personality not to be completely swamped by it, and the same can be said of Sullivan, at least in the Savoy operettas. But the influence of his weakest works, intensified by that of Gounod, degenerated into the most cloying qualities of late Victorian church music. In France, again via Gounod, it led to results that were healthier, because they were freer from pretensions to solemnity. Gounod himself was incapable of the power of the finest things in *Elijah*, and when he attempted to achieve it he failed lamentably, but his lyrical work, which owes much to Mendelssohn, is fresh and attractive, and echoes of it can be found in the music of Saint-Saëns, Bizet and Massenet. In some ways Mendelssohn and Saint-Saëns have most in common; both had an easy and natural lyric gift, and a love for what might be described as picturesquely religious effects. But, if

Mendelssohn did not wholly fulfil the promise of his early youth, it may reasonably be hoped that, had he lived to Saint-Saëns's age, he would not have produced so large a mass of lifelessly correct and conservative work. And in Saint-Saëns's music, for all its smoothness and suavity, there is often an inconsistency between his Gounodesque lyricism and his rather consciously academic counterpoint. Mendelssohn has sometimes been criticized for introducing a chorale at the climax of his Fugue in E minor from Op. 35, but the result has real dramatic power and a sense of inevitability; he could never have perpetrated a stylistic oddity like the prelude to Saint-Saëns's *Le Déluge*, where a four-part fugal exposition is followed by a very sentimental violin solo, as though the composer were saying, with a sigh of relief, 'Now I have done my counterpoint for the day and can enjoy myself.' For Mendelssohn counterpoint was a living language, and his fugal writing never has the air of cultivating deliberately the language of the past.

In Germany composers as dissimilar as Brahms, Mahler and Richard Strauss have all in various ways derived from Mendelssohn. Some of the greyer and more introspective of the Songs without Words, such as Op. 19, No. 5, Op. 102, No. 1, and the three gondola songs, are strongly prophetic of Brahms in their harmonic colour; some of Mahler's lyrical movements, such as the *Adagietto* from the fifth Symphony, are very Mendelssohnian, and there are many things in the music of Strauss, especially in the later operas, that strongly suggest Mendelssohn put under a large and powerful magnifying glass. Also, apart from the actual idiom of the music, there are several composers of the latter half of the nineteenth century who may well have learned something from Mendelssohn's skilful and smoothly polished workmanship: Saint-Saëns in France, Bruch in Germany, Glazunov in Russia and Stanford in England. At the time when Stanford was finding his feet as a composer Mendelssohn-worship was less rampant in England; it was easier to come under his influence without being overwhelmed by it, and for Stanford, consciously or not, it was probably a healthy corrective to his passionate devotion to Brahms, and helped him to achieve his remarkable skill in producing the maximum of sonority from a clear and economical texture.

Before proceeding to a detailed examination of Mendelssohn's music it is worth pausing for a few moments to consider how far it can be regarded as a reflection of the personality revealed in his everyday life. This is not by any means a foregone conclusion; it can be said of some of the greatest composers, notably Beethoven and Wagner, that the finest characteristics of their music were notably absent from their dealings with their fellow creatures. In the case of Mendelssohn there is a closer parallel between life and works, though they diverge now and again. To begin with less attractive characteristics, it is only too easy to find in the music equivalents to the rather pompously moralizing tone that was liable to appear in his letters and conversation; also his excessive restlessness is reflected in some of the *agitato* movements that seem to run feverishly about without achieving anything of note. On the other hand the finest of the scherzos seem not merely to echo the brilliance and liveliness of his demeanour, but to transfigure them, so that they acquire a new and wonderful imaginativeness. He was by no means incapable of losing his temper, and could do so in his music, but less frequently and sometimes with little effect; occasionally, however, as in the remarkable *Volkslied* from the fourth book of Songs without Words, it happens with astonishing fire and explosiveness. And in his music there are a few indications, such as the opening of the *Capriccio* in B flat minor for piano and the F minor string Quartet, of the very deep poignant emotion that he was certainly capable of feeling in his life, especially after the deaths of his parents and his sister. But there is one quality in his music that seems rather to stand aside from his daily life; it is what Professor Gerald Abraham, in *A Hundred Years of Music,* has described as 'the sweet, Virgilian purity of his idyllic passages.' It was quite often overladen with sentiment, but by no means invariably, and at its best it is full of a quietly idyllic serenity that seems to have played little part in Mendelssohn's everyday life, but adds a most attractive and frequently underestimated charm to his music.

CHAPTER VIII

PIANO AND ORGAN WORKS

ALTHOUGH Mendelssohn's piano music contains individual works that are very familiar, it is more varied in scale and mood than is often imagined. The Sonata in G minor, Op. 105, is the earliest of all his published works. It was finished in 1821, by which time Mendelssohn was already a prolific composer, and it is thoroughly fluent and sure of itself. In the first movement there are touches of chromatic colour reminiscent of Mozart, but the influence of Haydn is more pronounced, especially in the use of the same material for both first and second subjects. The ideas are not particularly distinguished, but they are handled with considerable resourcefulness. The finale is similar in style but simpler in texture; the *adagio*, though rather vague and impro-visatory in manner, is more imaginative than the rest of the Sonata, and more individual in feeling. But the prevailing impression left by the work as a whole is of an ease and assurance remarkable for a boy of eleven, preparing the way for the astonish-ing originality which was to appear a few years later.

The well-known *Andante and Rondo Capriccioso*, Op. 14, was probably written in 1824; if so, it was the most individual work that he had yet produced. It follows an unusual scheme that reappears on several later occasions in the piano works—a short slow movement in the major leading to a quick one in the minor. The luxuriant *andante* shows traces of the influence of Weber, but the rhythmic shape of the main melody, beginning on the third beat of the bar, is very personal:

Equally so is the brilliant and fairylike mood of the Rondo; the second theme is the weakest feature, but the piece as a whole is fresh and exhilarating, and well deserves its popularity. But in many ways the less known *Capriccio* in F sharp minor, Op. 5, is a work of greater distinction. This was written in the summer of 1825 and was highly thought of by Mendelssohn himself. Here there is less of the influence of Weber and more of that of Beethoven and Domenico Scarlatti; behind the mercurial brilliance of the piano writing there is a surprisingly fierce energy, especially in the trio and the coda, in both of which the phrase:

is worked very effectively against semiquaver counterpoints. The influence of Domenico Scarlatti, which was noted, not altogether to Mendelssohn's satisfaction, by Rossini, is an interesting feature in his style, and a healthy corrective to his more sentimental side. It can be seen in several of the *Seven Characteristic Pieces*, Op. 7, which are thought to have been written in 1825 at the latest, especially in the lively second piece, in B minor, and the sixth, in E minor, which has something of the pathos of Scarlatti's fine Sonata in B minor, No. 33 in Longo's edition. Counterpoint plays an important part in this set: the first piece has a flowing polyphonic texture throughout, and the third and fifth are fugues. These are both on a large scale; the third has touches of Scarlatti, both in its vivacity and in the occasional unorthodoxy of the part-writing, but the fifth is more suggestive of Bach. It is a serious, broadly constructed composition, full of academic devices, perhaps less personal than the later piano fugues, but of great dignity, and with a vivid sense of gradually increasing tension. But the fourth and seventh pieces of this set are the most wholly individual; the former, in A major, is a lively *moto perpetuo* in full sonata form, admirably constructed, with a passage of singular imaginativeness at the end of the development. The seventh is a brilliantly effective piece in Mendelssohn's most delicate and fairylike mood, strongly anticipating the atmosphere of the *Midsummer Night's Dream* overture; the very unexpected change to the minor key in the final bars is strangely impressive. The whole set is well worth the attention of pianists and should be better known. Probably about this time was written the curious Fantasia on *The Last Rose of Summer*, a flimsy composition in which Mendelssohn appears to become less and less interested in the Irish tune, and eventually floats into a pleasant but quite irrelevant final section that has no discoverable connection with what has preceded it.

The next piano work, the Sonata in E, Op. 6, was completed in March 1826. By this time Mendelssohn had written the Octet and three movements of the string Quintet in A, and this Sonata, though not quite up to the level of the two chamber works, is of considerable interest and attractiveness. The quietly flowing 6–8 tempo of the first movement suggests that of Beethoven's Op. 101, but the atmosphere is essentially Mendelssohnian. Themes of a singing, lyrical character are fitted with ease and spontaneity into sonata form, the development and coda being particularly imaginative. The second movement combines the tempo of a minuet with the mood of a scherzo and is of delightful quality; the subtle changes in its return after the trio are noteworthy. It is followed by an elaborate fugal recitative, culminating in arpeggios reminiscent of the first movement of Beethoven's Sonata in D minor. These lead to a short *andante* which might easily have been made into a complete movement, but is instead interrupted by a passage that recalls the first movement without quoting any of its main themes. These three incidents are all repeated, the recitative being curtailed, thereby increasing its intensity, and the passage from the first movement prolonged so as to lead straight into the finale. This is a high-spirited movement, with a touch of vulgarity in its themes, but developed with admirable gusto; after its final climax it subsides quietly into a further reminiscence of the first movement, quoting its main theme and also, with slight alterations, its coda. The idea of ending the first and final movements of a work with almost the same music was used a few years later by Mendelssohn in the string Quartet, Op. 12, and, over half a century later, by Brahms in his clarinet Quintet. The design of the E major Sonata, which is directed to be performed without a break between the movements, is most convincingly carried out, and is full of the freshness and poetry that are so characteristic of Mendelssohn's work of this period. His third sonata, in B flat, written a year later, has some interesting points of structure, but its musical invention is on a far lower level. It is ironical that it should have been published posthumously as Op. 106, as the opening of its first movement is absurdly suggestive of a comfortable and domestic version of Beethoven's 'Hammerklavier' Sonata, and this comparison is further emphasized by the fact that it modulates to G major for its second subject and contains a fugal episode in its development. The second subject itself, however, is more reminiscent of the *Coriolan* overture, the influence of which is to be found in other works by Mendelssohn. The short scherzo that follows has more character, though it is decidedly awkward to play; the *andante* is a pleasant but rather insipid barcarolle. The finale is approached by a bridge passage that contains allusions to the first movement and interrupted towards the end by a reminiscence of the scherzo; it suffers, like the opening *allegro,* from an inability to move at anything more exciting than an imperturbable amble. It is hard to believe that this disappointingly pedestrian work was written in the same year as the string Quartet in A minor and the fine Fugue in E minor that was published ten years later in Op. 35.

Of the three *Fantasias or Caprices* composed in 1829 the second, a very imaginative scherzo, and the third, a gently flowing Song without Words, are both very successful; the first begins and ends impressively, in the manner of the first movement of the 'Scottish'

Symphony, but the central portion is rather commonplace. The return to the opening mood, as so often with Mendelssohn, is beautifully contrived. The *Fantasia* in F sharp minor, Op. 28, sometimes referred to by Mendelssohn as the 'Scottish' Sonata, was written before 1830; it is an interesting work in three movements, of which the first, in slow tempo, is preceded and several times interrupted by a rhapsodical introductory passage. The stormy and grandiose return of its highly characteristic main theme:

and its final unharmonized reappearance are both very impressive. The second movement is an amiable little scherzo, opening with a slightly Schubertian phrase; the finale is a fiery and impetuous movement in sonata form. In this work, as elsewhere, the key of F sharp minor seems to have stimulated Mendelssohn to an unusually high level of intensity. The three *Capriccios*, Op. 33, are more unequal. The second, in E major, is a demurely ambling movement in 6-8 time, conventional in its themes, but with attractive details; its influence may be found in much of Sterndale Bennett's music. The other two are in Mendelssohn's familiar 'agitato' mood, but it somehow fails to catch fire; their most notable features are their slow introductions and indeed that of the third *Capriccio*, in B flat minor, is one of the most distinguished passages in all the piano works:

After the sombre solemnity of this the main section of the movement, though quite effective, seems fussy and trivial. The

Capriccio in E minor, Op. 110, and the *Andante Cantabile and Presto Agitato*, both dating from the late 1830s, follow the plan of the *Andante and Rondo Capriccioso*—a lively movement in the minor key being preceded by a slow introduction in the major. The latter is the more attractive, but neither is of special interest. On the other hand the *Scherzo a Capriccio* in F sharp minor is a wholly admirable composition in which the usual scherzo-like brilliance is tempered by an unexpected undercurrent of melancholy. The three Preludes and the three Studies eventually published as Op. 104 *a* and *b* vary in quality. The first and third Preludes are of ceremonial character and not of great interest; the second, in B minor, has the air of being a preliminary sketch for the E minor Prelude from Op. 35. The same may be said of the first Study, in B flat minor, which has a broad and attractive melody; the second is dull and over-long, but the third, in A minor, has a pleasant impishness resulting from persistent 'wrong notes' which might well have shocked some of Mendelssohn's more conservative friends. The six easy little *Christmas Pieces* composed some years later in London have freshness and charm, though the fourth, in D, contains some unfortunate instances of Mendelssohn's tendency to hold up the rhythm of a passage by breaking rather complacently into block harmony for a bar or so. Other isolated pieces include two *Musical Sketches* in B flat and G minor, a Study in F minor and a very short Scherzo in B minor, which are all of pleasant quality.

But of far greater importance than any of these are the six Preludes and Fugues, Op. 35, the composition of which covered a number of years, the fugue in every case being written first. Of the well-known pair in E minor the prelude, written in 1837, is similar in texture and general plan to many of the Songs without Words, a number of which had already been composed, but it has a melody of great vigour and a most exhilarating impetuosity. The fugue, which dates from 1827, has something of the gradual increase of tension that Mendelssohn had produced, in a more academic and less personal style, in the Fugue in A from Op. 7. Here, however, there is far more agitation, and after an almost feverish climax a chorale melody enters in the major over a moving bass; finally it ends with a quiet reminiscence of the fugue subject. The whole conception is most original and convincingly carried out, with a full realization of the dramatic possibilities of counterpoint. Of the other preludes and fugues the most striking is the fifth, in F minor. Here the prelude is again of the Song without Words type, but slow and melancholy in mood, with poignant harmonic effects and a melody of considerable beauty that frequently reappears in unexpected ways. The fugue has remarkable drive and energy, and its general atmosphere is not unlike that of the finale of the *Fantasia* in F sharp minor. The Prelude in B minor is a delightful *moto perpetuo* scherzo and the fugue robust and rather Handelian in character. The Preludes and Fugues in D and A flat are less striking, but contain much pleasant, placidly flowing music and are free from the rather oversweet flavour that slightly spoils the concluding bars of the E minor fugue. The A flat prelude is similar in general idea to the slightly earlier *Duet* Song without Words in the same key, but is more interesting in texture, as the two voices sing contrapuntally, whereas in the Song without Words they are for the most part either antiphonal or in octaves. The Prelude and Fugue in B flat are the most brightly coloured of the set; the prelude has a broad melody and a slightly ponderous nobility of manner and the fugue, though more superficial than some of the others, has great brilliance. In the fugues the part-writing is conceived essentially in terms of the keyboard and would not be easy to score into separate parts, but there can be no doubt of its effectiveness for the medium for which it was written. The subjects are always admirably suited to their purpose, and Mendelssohn shows here a power of employing a contrapuntal style without any loss of individuality or suggestion of the sham-antique. And though the preludes are predominantly harmonic in texture, they quite often contain suggestions of counterpoint that bring them very happily into line with the fugues. In addition to Op. 35 there is another Prelude and Fugue in E minor, of which the fugue was written in 1827 and the prelude in 1841; the fugue is the more interesting of the two, but neither reaches the level of Op. 35.

The three sets of variations for piano were all written in 1841, in a mood of great enthusiasm. The first set, the *Variations sérieuses* in D minor, Op. 54, is by far the best. The theme has great beauty and pathos; in some of the variations the harmonic scheme is altered considerably, but the most important features of the melodic outline are usually maintained. The keyboard writing is very varied and resourceful; the fourth variation, with its two-part canonic writing, the fugal tenth and the very Schumannesque eleventh are particularly attractive. The rather anthem-like atmosphere of the fourteenth does not continue long enough to become oppressive, but provides quite an effective contrast in its surroundings, and in the final variation and coda the tension is most effectively maintained. The other two sets are pleasant but a good deal less distinguished. Op. 82, in E flat, has a theme that is the considerably superior prototype of many Victorian hymn-tunes, and the whole set is for the most part bathed in an atmosphere of good-tempered sabbatical placidity. The third set, in B flat, has rather more variety, but is spoilt by a distressingly commonplace finale; it was afterwards rewritten, with some additional variations, for piano duet. The only other work for this medium is an *Allegro brillant* of little importance. Of the works mentioned in this chapter two of the best, the Prelude and Fugue in E minor and the *Variations sérieuses*, are played fairly frequently. But there are others, such as the *Seven Characteristic Pieces*, the Sonata in E, the *Fantasia* in F sharp minor, the *Capriccio* in the same key and some of the other preludes and fugues, that are surprisingly unfamiliar and well worthy of attention.

There remain for discussion the Songs without Words, of

which six books appeared in Mendelssohn's lifetime and two posthumously. These pieces contributed enormously to his popularity, especially in England; they have been both praised and belittled indiscriminately at various times, but at this distance it is possible to have a more balanced view of them. If they are put beside the piano lyrics of Mendelssohn's contemporaries Chopin and Schumann, it can be seen at once that they move in a far more ordered and limited world, sheltered from the disturbingly intense passions of the other two. Even in the most deeply felt pieces the emotions hardly ever overstep the limits of politeness, and there is little that can be described as adventurous or breath-taking. But against these limitations can be set many excellent qualities. In these pieces it can never be felt, as in some of Mendelssohn's larger works, that the material is being subjected to a strain greater than it is able to bear; the keyboard writing, though unassuming, is always effective within its limits, and the forms are neatly rounded. There is abundant invention of unobtrusive but individual accompaniment figures, and the melodies, though they have a certain sameness, are always shapely and flowing. The first book, Op. 19, which is one of the best, contains instances of the different types of piece that are liable to recur throughout the series. The first two are lyrics of considerable beauty, the one serene and the other plaintive in mood; the third, sometimes known as the *Hunting Song*, shows how Mendelssohn's attempts to gallop are liable to degenerate into a comfortable jog-trot. The next is the earliest example of a class of piece to be found in every book but one, consisting of a simply harmonized melody preceded by a short introduction that is repeated at the end. The present specimen, though its polite Sunday morning atmosphere may now seem rather smug, is very characteristic and, in its way, effective. The two remaining pieces have an attractively grey and sombre colouring; the fifth, with the familiar direction *agitato,* is a thoughtful movement in sonata form, and the sixth is the well-known *Gondola Song* in G minor.

The first piece of the second book, Op. 30, is a flowing lyrical movement similar to that of the first, but richer in colour, with a very beautiful return to the main theme. The second is the counterpart of No. 3 in Book I, a lively galloping movement with considerably more fire and excitement than its predecessor. The third follows in the steps of the fourth from the earlier book and is weighed down by a rich and cloying sentimentality. No. 4, like the fifth from Book I, is in sonata form, and is one of the best of the whole series; the second theme, with its restless tonality, is unusually passionate, and the coda, in which the hammering accompaniment gradually subsides, most impressive. The fifth has no obvious counterpart in Book I; it is a quiet and unassuming little piece with subtle and attractive details, and its placid but quite unsentimental mood is not unlike the second Prelude from Op. 35. The second book, like the first, ends with a *Gondola Song*; less immediately attractive than the earlier piece, it improves greatly with acquaintance and the return, at a climax, of a phrase from the introductory passage is remarkably effective.

Despite the weakness of individual pieces the general level of the first two books of Songs without Words is decidedly high; that of the third, Op. 38, is lower. No. 1 has less character than the corresponding pieces in the two earlier books, though it has charming moments. No. 2 begins attractively but is spoilt by a weak and repetitive second theme. The third piece is brightly coloured, and exhilarating to play, but the fourth, similar in design to No. 4 in Book I and No. 3 in Book II, is comfortable rather than inspired. The two remaining pieces have far more value; the agitation of the fifth is admirably sustained by the movement of the bass and the *Duet* has great charm, though, as has been already pointed out, the idea was carried out with more enterprise in the slightly later Prelude in A flat. The fourth book, Op. 53, has two weak numbers, the fourth, which is over-sentimental, and the sixth, which has an ingeniously contrived accompaniment, but a disappointingly commonplace tune over it. The remaining four, however, are all good in their different ways. The first is in a very tender mood, expressed with delight-fully clear texture, and a flowing, barcarolle-like measure, and the second has an attractive, rather Schumannesque warmth and im-pulsiveness. A comparison of its main theme with that of the third piece from Book III is of interest (both are quoted on p. 153); there is an obvious surface resemblance between them, but the later tune has more character than the earlier and is treated with far more resource. The third, despite a certain rhythmic monotony, is pianistically very effective, but the most remarkable piece in the book is the fifth. Here the plan first used in the fourth piece in Book I is expanded to a far larger scale and the introductory matter is not content with reappearing at the end but also inter-rupts the melody several times. The harmonic colour has none of Mendelssohn's usual suavity, and its roughness culminates with the cadence:

The whole piece is worth noting as one of the rare occasions on which Mendelssohn exchanged his normal polite manners for something more aggressive. The fifth book, Op. 62, opens with the usual quietly flowing lyric; it is one of the best of its kind, with an attractive insistence on the harmony of the dominant seventh. The second piece, marked *allegro con fuoco*, will always suggest to the present writer the exuberant chatter of Jane Austen's Miss Bates. The next two are strongly contrasted in mood the, third being a sombre and dignified funeral march and the fourth showing Mendelssohn at his most comfortably urbane, but in both are to be found harmonic clashes of an unexpected kind.

They are followed by the last and most beautiful of the three *Gondola Songs*, which is curiously prophetic of certain things by Brahms, such as the song *Meerfahrt*. Of the much hackneyed *Spring Song* it is difficult to say much now except that it has withstood over a hundred years of maltreatment with remarkable fortitude and still retains a considerable degree of period charm.

A similar piece concludes the sixth book, Op. 67, the rest of which is, however, of more distinctive quality. It opens with a thoughtful and polished lyric, with attractive and unexpected details; this is followed by a lively *staccato* piece of earlier date than the others, and similar in mood to the B minor Prelude from Op. 35. The third piece is, in its quiet way, one of the most individual; it is in a serene and cloistered atmosphere that is, however, completely free from sentimentality. No. 4 is the admirable and very original little scherzo whose merits have sometimes been obscured by irrelevant and unnecessary descriptive titles.[1] The fifth has a singular and haunting pathos; in its introductory phrase:

there is a curious foretaste of Grieg. This was the last book of Songs without Words to be published in Mendelssohn's lifetime, and its two successors are both on a lower level. The seventh, Op. 85, is the weakest of them all, though it contains one remarkable piece, the very terse and reticent No. 2, which is earlier than the rest. The others are of a more ordinary type, though the fourth has a pleasant nostalgic charm and the sixth a rather engaging gentility. On the other hand the third is regrettably

[1] In a letter written to Marc-André Souchay in 1842, Mendelssohn expressed distrust of titles of this kind on the ground that they are essentially matters of personal reaction, and that the emotions aroused by music are too subtle to be tied down by any extra-musical suggestions.

vulgar, one of the worst of the whole collection. The eighth book, Op. 102, can be divided into three groups; the weakest are the second and sixth, which both suffer from a sickly religiosity, particularly the former. The third and fifth, which were apparently written on the same day, are gay and unassuming, and look back to the mood of the *Christmas Pieces*. As so often, the best pieces are the two in minor keys. The fourth is notable for the attractively unsettled tonality of its main theme, and the first is rich and sombre in colouring, with a haunting second theme:

echoes of which recur in the first movements of the C minor Trio and the violin Concerto. A vigorous and interesting piece in D minor, obviously intended for one of the posthumous books, was published recently, with an arrangement by Ernest Walker of a charming unpublished song *Im Kahn* and a short canon. With all their limitations and inequalities these eight books of Songs without Words contain much that is not only superficially attractive but possessed of real distinction, and it is interesting to learn that Busoni, whose attitude towards music became more and more formidably critical, began to practise them with enthusiasm towards the end of his life, and that a copy of them was found open on his piano when he died.

Of Mendelssohn's organ works the three Preludes and Fugues, Op. 37, were published in the same year as the set for piano and had been composed during the same period. They are less varied in texture and perhaps less striking thematically, but contain much admirable music. The best is the first, in C minor, in which the prelude has a finely sustained flow, and the fugue a firmness of outline and melodic vigour which save it from the amiable jog-trot into which Mendelssohn is liable to fall when writing in 12-8 time. The second, in G, is more placid in mood, the prelude being in an attractively pastoral vein. The

Prelude and Fugue in D minor are less happily balanced; the prelude is over-long, and its contrapuntal sections are too similar to the fugue for the latter to make its effect.

The six organ Sonatas, Op. 65, were written some years later, in response to a request for organ music from the English pub-lishers Coventry & Hollier. The pieces were originally to be described as voluntaries, but eventually Mendelssohn grouped them together as sonatas, though they bear little relation to the traditional sonata form. The first, in F minor, is on the whole the most varied; its opening movement consists largely of fugal writing, interspersed with developments of the chorale 'Ich hab' in Gottes Herz und Sinn.' A quiet *adagio,* similar in character to many of the Songs without Words, is followed by an interesting recitative that seems at the same time to look back to the early piano Sonata in E major and forward to certain things of César Franck; it leads eventually into an exhilarating toccata-like finale. The second Sonata contains nothing on so large a scale. A short introduction leads to a delicately contrapuntal *adagio*; the third movement, also short, is of processional character and is followed by a thoughtful and closely wrought fugue. The third Sonata opens with what is probably the most distinguished movement in these works. After a dignified introductory section, a long fugue is worked with splendid resourcefulness and sustained tension, the chorale 'Aus tiefer Not' being introduced in the pedal part. The general atmosphere is not unlike that of the great E minor piano fugue from Op. 35, and there is the same gradual increase of speed. Eventually the introduction returns, the fugue subject being ingeniously recalled towards the end. After this, the short Song without Words which closes the Sonata, though pleasant enough in itself, seems something of an anticlimax. The first and last movements of the fourth Sonata, in B flat, are among the most brightly coloured. In the former the quick, brilliant figures with which the movement opens are eventually worked contrapuntally with the more solid theme of the central section, the whole scheme being not unlike that of the elaborate Prelude in E flat from the first book of Bach's 'Forty-eight.' The finale on the other hand opens with a solid and dignified theme which returns at the end, but the greater part of the movement is a fugue on an ingenious subject:

Allegro vivace e maestoso

which seems at once to suggest the sound of organ pedals. The two central movements are more unpretentious; the second is not of great interest, but the third has a pleasant lyrical flow and an attractive clarity of texture. The fifth Sonata opens with a chorale, the melody of which appears to be Mendelssohn's own; it is followed first by a kind of barcarolle and then by a more extended finale. For the most part the movements of these sonatas seem to have been written as independent pieces and subsequently grouped together by their composer, but the sixth Sonata, in D minor, has more unity. A set of variations on the chorale 'Vater unser im Himmelreich' is followed by a simple but very expressive fugue on the first line of the chorale, and the sonata ends, like the third, with a short Song without Words. The result is here far more satisfactory; the opening bars of the finale grow out of the cadence of the fugue, giving a feeling of continuity, and after the unbroken minor tonality of the first two movements the change to the major for the third is very attractive. Apart from the sonatas and the preludes and fugues, there are several organ works by Mendelssohn that have remained in manuscript. These include some pieces written in the early 1820s, three fugues, one of which was eventually used in the second Sonata, and two pieces written in 1844, an Andante in F and an Allegro in D minor.

CHAPTER IX

CHAMBER MUSIC

THE earliest surviving specimen of Mendelssohn's chamber music is the piano Quartet in C minor, Op. 1, which dates from the autumn of 1822. Compared with the still earlier piano Sonata in G minor, it shows less of the influence of Haydn and more of that of Mozart and Weber. The opening of the first movement suggests Mozart's piano Sonata in the same key, and there is a strong flavour of Weber in the gaily operatic second subject. The reference to the opening phrase towards the end of the exposition is a procedure very characteristic of Mendelssohn. The thematic invention is still undistinguished, and the finale is built on a single, rather dull theme which serves for both first and second subject. On the other hand the modulations in both the first two movements are often extremely effective. The mercurial vivacity of the scherzo looks ahead to later things; its trio is curiously scored for viola, cello and the pianist's left hand.

The following year Mendelssohn wrote three chamber works: the piano Quartet, Op. 2, the violin Sonata, Op. 4, both in F minor, and a string Quartet in E flat which was published only in 1879. Of these the violin Sonata has one or two unusual touches, such as the opening recitative and the unexpectedly quiet end of the finale, but is on the whole the weakest and most colourless of all Mendelssohn's chamber works. The string Quartet has far more individuality and handles this very sensitive medium with remarkable ease and fluency. There is a distinctly personal flavour in the opening bars of the first movement:

and some pleasantly unexpected touches occur, as at the beginning of the coda. The *adagio*, rather square rhythmically, is in an elegiac mood that was expressed with greater distinction a few years later in the slow movement of the Octet. The minuet is Mozart-like, but the trio has a thoroughly individual flavour, and the finale, a lively fugue on three subjects, shows a wealth of contrapuntal ingenuity that is remarkable for a composer who had just passed his fourteenth birthday. The piano Quartet in F minor, written towards the end of the same year, is on the whole less interesting, though its scoring is an advance on that of its predecessor. The first movement and finale are over-long for their material, and both suffer, particularly the latter, from an excess of empty passage work. The *adagio*, though still rather conventional in its themes, has some attractive colouring and modulations, but the most individual part of the work is un-doubtedly the lyrical intermezzo, which foreshadows many later things, though the length of its coda makes its structure rather lopsided.

The Sextet in D for piano, string quartet and double bass, composed in the spring of 1824, is an interesting but disconcert-ingly unequal work. The first movement contains some pleasant ideas, but they are usually drowned in a flood of conventionally brilliant bravura work, and the finale, with its polka-like rhythms, is still more vapid. The slow movement is more individual, though the chromaticisms are sometimes reminiscent of Spohr, but the maturest part of the work is the so-called minuet, in D minor, an agitated movement in 6–8 time, the theme of which returns in a massive and extended form near the end of the finale, producing a climax of considerable power. After this material from the finale reappears, rather effectively, in the minor key, the major not being re-established till the final bars.

The piano Quartet in B minor, Op. 3, which was begun in 1824 and finished during the following year, is a far more consistent work. The material has greater breadth and the Weberian exuberance of the piano writing is more controlled. In both the first and last movements the main theme is followed by another that is also in the tonic minor, but soon reappears in the relative major for the second subject. The slow movement recalls Spohr in its luxuriant chromaticism, but has an attractive variety of phrase-lengths. But, again, it is in the scherzo that the maturest music is to be found. Here, as in the slightly later *Capriccio* for piano in F sharp minor, the vivacious 3–8 rhythm saves the rapid passages from the slightest suspicion of emptiness, and in both movements there is a strong foretaste of the scherzo from the *Midsummer Night's Dream* music. Just before the end of the finale there is a very effective allusion to the theme of the first movement. Of the chamber works that Mendelssohn had so far written, this has the most intensity, and it might still be worth revival.

But, with all its fine points, it is easily outshone by the Octet for strings, Op. 20, which was written in the same year and still remains one of the freshest and most original works that Mendelssohn ever wrote. The medium had been used, in a mild and scholarly style, by Spohr in his double quartets, during which the two groups of strings are frequently treated antiphonally. Mendelssohn showed that he was fully capable of doing this when occasion demanded, but for a great deal of the work he employs a frankly orchestral texture, and the splendid opening of the first movement has a sweep and exhilaration which he sometimes tried, only with partial success, to recapture in later years. It is exuberant, imaginative and full of incident, one of the most remarkable features being the way in which the melody of the second subject:

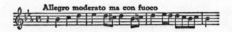

Allegro moderato ma con fuoco

which could so easily have introduced a languid and incongruous atmosphere, is always prevented from doing this by some new contrapuntal detail. The treatment of sonata form, as so often in Mendelssohn's early works, is decidedly free, especially in the recapitulation. The *andante* is of an unusual type, less obviously melodious than the average Mendelssohn slow movement, and sometimes showing the influence of the latest works of Mozart, particularly in the attractively clashing lines in thirds that occur in the second subject. The colouring is here less orchestral than in the first movement and beautifully graded. The scherzo, in very terse sonata form, evokes the fairylike mood of the *Rondo Capriccioso* for piano and the third movement of the third piano Quartet with exquisite delicacy and lightness of touch; it is one of the most perfect things Mendelssohn ever wrote, the beautifully contrived lull in the harmonic movement just before the re-capitulation being particularly characteristic. The finale is full of lively contrapuntal writing, with an amusing contrast between the rapid first subject and the stolidly tramping phrase that follows it; at one point the opening theme of the scherzo is recalled, and in the coda the music, without losing its vivacity, gradually increases in breadth. The whole work shows a mastery astonishing in a boy of sixteen, and it is full of a singular kind of wayward billiance that he never surpassed.

The string Quintet in A, Op. 18, was composed in 1826, but its original second movement, a minuet, was eventually discarded in favour of a slow intermezzo composed in 1832 in memory of Mendelssohn's friend Eduard Rietz. It is a milder, less adventurous work than the Octet, but contains much excellent music. The first movement opens with a delightful, rather Mozartian theme:

Allegro con moto

On the formal side it is leisurely to a fault; a prominent phrase in the exposition is omitted entirely in the recapitulation; yet the whole movement runs to considerable length and, with all its great charm, leaves a certain impression of diffuseness. The slow movement, though written six years later, fits well with the rest of the work. Opening with a characteristically Mendelssohnian 'fingerprint':

it is pleasantly warm and rich in colouring, with enough rhythmic impulse and contrapuntal interest to save it from becoming over-sentimental. The scherzo is very similar in mood to that of the Octet, and hardly less successful; it contains, however, more fugal writing, and its atmosphere of fairylike mystery is interrupted now and then by rude explosions. The finale has an obvious resemblance to that of Beethoven's string Quartet in F, Op. 18, No. 1; it is admirably fresh and vivacious, though perhaps less individual than the other movements. The whole work is, however, worthy of far more attention than it receives at the present time.

Two very dissimilar works for string quartet were written in 1827. The Fugue in E flat, published many years later as part of Op. 81, is a thoughtful, quietly flowing piece of writing, similar in general mood to the piano Fugue in A flat from Op. 35. Slightly earlier than this is the Quartet in A minor, which was published several years later as Op. 13. This is of exceptional interest as showing how deeply Mendelssohn was affected at the time by the later works of Beethoven. The phrase in the introduction that he quotes from his own song *Ist es wahr?*:

suggests the central movement of Beethoven's Sonata, 'Les

Adieux'; the main theme of the first movement has a strong likeness to that of his A minor Quartet, Op. 132; the fugal passage in the slow movement looks back to the *allegretto* of the F minor Quartet, Op. 95, the recitative at the beginning of the finale to a similar passage in that of Op. 132, and the closing bars of the final coda to those of the cavatina from Op. 130. But, these observations made, it is only fair to add that Mendelssohn's A minor Quartet is very far from being a mere succession of reminiscences. The influence of Beethoven was not always beneficial to him, and his attempts to emulate the dignity and serenity of such things as the slow movements of the choral Symphony and the Trio, Op. 97, are usually unsuccessful; but here it is for the most part the more restless, passionate side of Beethoven that is affecting him, and the results, for all their indebtedness, have real vitality and individuality. The first movement has a remarkable intensity; particularly impressive features are the quiet, reflective passage that ends the development and the stormy coda that culminates unexpectedly with a familiar operatic formula. The slow movement, curiously marked *Adagio non lento,* is deeply thoughtful and full of incident. The charming intermezzo has far less Beethoven influence than the rest of the work; it is more lyrical than the scherzos of the Octet and the A major Quintet, but has a central section of fairylike vivacity, with delightful contrasts of colour. The finale, opening dramatically with a recitative, is in sonata form, the development recalling both this recitative and the fugal theme from the slow movement; this returns once more in the coda, after which the introductory *adagio* of the first rounds off the work very satisfactorily, the references to *Ist es wahr?* being more prolonged than before.

Two chamber works date from 1829, the *Variations concertantes* in D for cello and piano, Op. 17, and the string Quartet in E flat, Op. 12. The former, written for his brother Paul, is built on an attractive theme; the variations, as often with Mendelssohn, are very free, though the second part of the melody is adhered to more closely than the first. Both instruments are given music of considerable brilliance, and the work as a whole is thoroughly effective, though not of great depth. The E flat Quartet is smoother and more lyrical in style than the A minor, and the influence of Beethoven is less noticeable, though the slow introduction to the first movement is similar in general atmosphere to that of Beethoven's Op. 74. But the *allegro* that follows is entirely Mendelssohnian, and, as in the first movement of the E major piano Sonata, material of a flowing, song-like character fits into sonata form without any feeling of strain. An unusual feature is the haunting new theme that appears in the development and reappears not only in the coda but also in the finale. The general plan of this Quartet has much in common with that of the E major Sonata, and in both cases it is affected by the predominantly lyrical character of the first movement. The well-known and delightful canzonetta of the Quartet is decidedly similar in mood to the minuet of the Sonata. The *andante* of the Quartet is more conventional than the very remarkable third movement of the Sonata, but it is shorter than usual and twice breaks into a recitative-like passage labelled *con fuoco*. The finale, following without a break, is a spirited movement, the greater part of which is in the relative minor. The theme that was first introduced at the beginning of the development section of the first movement reappears at a similar point here and finally, in the coda, it leads to an almost exact repetition of the coda of the first movement. Apart from the *Hymn of Praise*, this is the last instance in Mendelssohn's output of a work in which material is transferred from one movement to another (the E flat Quartet from Op. 44 may be considered a border-line case). On the whole Mendelssohn's approach to sonata form became increasingly orthodox in his later years.

The next chamber work is the set of two *Concertstücke* for clarinet, basset-horn and piano, written in 1833. These both contain three sections which contrast in mood like the movements of a sonata, but follow each other without a break and are not in sonata form. The style is pleasant, strongly influenced by Weber, and has little individuality. Far more interesting are the three string Quartets, Op. 44, of which the earliest is the work in E minor, composed in 1837 and published as No. 2 of the set. The most obvious feature of its first move‑ ment is the strong likeness to that of the violin Concerto, ideas for which began to occur to Mendelssohn soon afterwards, though it was not completed till some years later. In cases of this kind it quite often happens that the earlier work is the fresher of the two; here, however, the first movement of the E minor Quartet, with all its good qualities, has not quite the irresistible urge of that of the violin Concerto. The two main themes, though both attractive, are too similar in their rhythmic shape, and the rapid semiquaver passages are apt to be fussy. As so often, some of the most imaginative music comes at the end of the development, the return of the first theme being contrived with Mendelssohn's usual skill. The scherzo is wholly delightful and beautifully scored; the slow movement is similar to many of the Songs without Words, with a pleasantly flowing accompaniment and a gentle pace that, as the composer himself has directed, should not be dragged. The finale is lively and vigorous, with a broad and attractive second theme:

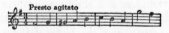

The Quartet in E flat, though less often played than the other two, is in many ways the most interesting of the three. Its first movement is one of Mendelssohn's longest, with an unusually incisive main theme, admirably suited for development, and several well contrasted secondary ideas, one of which recalls rhythmically the first movement of Beethoven's Quartet in C, Op. 59, No. 3 Finer still is the scherzo, which is deeply char‑ acteristic in its blend of vivacity and imaginativeness, a number of ideas, all in minor keys, being woven into an exquisitely light and delicate texture. The slow movement is more serious in character than that of the E minor Quartet; the harmony of the opening theme:

gives it a decidedly poignant flavour, and the part-writing is often beautifully clear. The finale, the main theme of which may or may not be derived from an accessory idea in the *adagio,* is brilliant but far more superficial than the rest, and weakens the general effect of what would otherwise have been one of the best of Mendelssohn's chamber works. His own favourite of this set, however, appears to have been the Quartet in D, which was written last. The first movement, which is on as large a scale as that of the E flat Quartet, is full of gusto and high spirits, with very individual themes, but it needs a full orchestra to do it justice. On the other hand the two central movements are among the most delicate that Mendelssohn ever wrote. The usual scherzo is replaced by a quiet and thoughtful minuet, similar in mood to that of Beethoven's Quartet in D from Op. 18; the flowing semiquavers of the trio, which return in the coda, supply just the right amount of contrast. The *andante* has points in common with that of the 'Italian' Symphony, though without its suggestions of a procession; it is a movement of great charm, gently pathetic in mood and beautifully written for its medium. The finale is rather commonplace in its ideas, and in such phrases as:

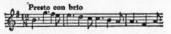

the rhythm is apt to amble; but its workmanship is admirable, with happy incidental touches, such the different ways in which the opening theme is harmonized in all its later appearances.

Looking back for a moment at this set of quartets as a whole, there can be little doubt that the E flat rises the highest, especially in its first two movements, but they all three contain excellent music and are far from deserving their present neglect.

Soon after these quartets came the cello and piano Sonata in B flat, Op. 45, which was written for Mendelssohn's brother Paul. This is a very pleasant and equable work, most gratefully written for the two instruments. Of its three movements the second grows mainly from a short rhythmic phrase, an unusual feature for a Mendelssohn *andante*; it is in a half melancholy, half playful mood and beautifully polished in design. Of the other two, which are almost too alike in atmosphere, the first is the stronger; the finale has a broad and attractive main theme, but the intervening episodes have rather the air of 'marking time.' As usual, however, the returns of the theme and the quiet coda are very successful. In 1839 came the Trio in D minor for piano and strings, which immediately achieved wide popularity. There are obvious reasons for this: it is vigorous, tuneful and very grateful to play. But in the two outer movements the material is not always strong enough for its treatment; the two themes of the first movement are very agreeable in themselves and would do admirably for songs, with or without words, but on several occasions, when they are played *fortissimo* in octaves, they seem to be invested with a publicity for which they are not suited. On the other hand the more lyrical and contrapuntal passages, including much of the development, are thoroughly successful. The *andante* is similar to several of the Songs without Words, especially the first of Book VI; the structure of the first theme, with two strains given out by the piano and repeated by the strings, suggests the *andante* of Beethoven's Trio in B flat, Op. 97; but the music itself is essentially Mendelssohnian, showing his lyrical manner at its pleasantest. The scherzo is gay and sparkling, and perhaps the most completely successful part of the work. The finale is very effective, but the piano part is over-brilliant, and the rhythm of the first theme, though impressive at first, is afterwards worked with a rather excessive persistence.

Some years elapsed before the next chamber work appeared, the cello Sonata in D, Op. 58, which at the same time rises higher and sinks lower than its predecessor. The first movement has an obvious similarity of mood to that of the 'Italian' Symphony, but the ideas have not quite the same freshness, the second subject being one of Mendelssohn's least distinguished. But they are treated with much energy and resourcefulness, with some impressive moments of reflection in the development and coda. The best music of the sonata is to be found in the two central movements, of which the second is a demure and highly polished scherzo of great charm. The short *adagio* is one of Mendelssohn's most original; a dignified, chorale-like melody is played by the piano and answered by the cello with an impassioned recitative; finally the two are combined. After this fine movement the facile and vapidly brilliant finale brings a disappointing anticlimax.

The second Trio, in C minor, was completed in 1845. Its first movement is considerably stronger than that of the D minor Trio, the themes being far more suitable for sonata form, particularly the very flexible opening phrase:

echoes of which occur in the finale of Brahms's piano Quartet in C minor. The second subject has a fine breadth, its first appearance and the brief allusion to it in the coda being particularly effective. The influence of Beethoven's *Coriolan* overture can be felt in this movement; the method of announcing the theme of the *andante* again looks back to the same master's 'Archduke' Trio, and this is emphasized by the fact that in both movements the two strains of the theme are played by the piano in rich block harmony. But the comparison also shows the great difference between Beethoven's solemn and dignified rhythm and Mendelssohn's contented amble, though this is less noticeable once the strings have entered. On the whole this movement is less attractive than the *andante* of the D minor Trio. Between the scherzos it is not easy to choose, though that of the C minor Trio is perhaps the more imaginative. Here the fairy-like atmosphere of the scherzos of the Octet and the A major Quintet is recaptured very happily, without any loss of freshness. The finale has a fine and passionate main theme and a rather commonplace second subject. The central episode introduces a chorale-like melody which is very impressive at its quiet first appearance, but its grandiose return in the coda needs a more massive medium. This is an interesting and ambitious movement, not on the same level as the opening *allegro,* but far above the finale of the D minor Trio.

The string Quintet in B flat, Op. 87, which was written later in 1845, is a tantalizingly unequal work. The opening of the first movement is an obvious attempt to recapture the atmosphere of the Octet; there is a strong similarity of outline between the two themes, but the surging exuberance of the Octet has here given place to something stiffer and more pompous. The triplet figure that occurs later in the first movement of the Quintet had also been used less feverishly but with more effect in the B flat cello Sonata. The best part of the movement is the ingenious treatment of the second subject. The *andante scherzando* that follows is on a far higher level; it is a rather more lyrical and sensitive relation of the second movement of the D major cello Sonata, and is more happily devised for its medium than the rest of the work. The *adagio* opens with a fine theme that seems to look at once backward to the slow movement of Beethoven's Quartet in F, Op. 59, No. 1, and forward to that of Brahms's String Quintet in G:

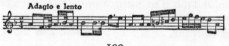

Adagio e lento

It does not quite fulfil the promise of its opening; there is an unnecessarily elaborate accompaniment for the first violin at the return of the main theme, and the coda, with its effective modulation to D major, is essentially orchestral in texture. But though uneven in inspiration it is of far higher quality than the finale, which expends its energy on thoroughly trivial material, and was not rated highly by Mendelssohn himself.

With the exception of a pleasant *Song without Words* for cello and piano the remaining chamber works are all for string quartet. First comes the *Capriccio* in E minor, written in 1843 and published as part of Op. 81. This is a spirited fugal movement preceded by a lyrical introduction; it has great vigour and is far removed from the traditional idea of Mendelssohn the polite drawingroom composer. Of still greater intensity, however, is the Quartet in F minor, Op. 80, which dates from 1847, the year of Mendelssohn's death. Regarded purely as quartet writing, this is not a good work; and it seems more than any of the others to cry out for a more spacious medium. But the undercurrent of restless agitation that is to be found in so many of the earlier works here rises to the surface in a remarkable manner. At the opening of the first movement there is an obvious suggestion of Beethoven's F minor Quartet, Op. 95, which was a special favourite of Mendelssohn's, but there is none of Beethoven's dour reticence. The lyrical relief provided by the second subject is very transitory, the return to the recapitulation is one of the most powerful passages that Mendelssohn ever wrote and the coda introduces a new theme with curiously compelling effect. The second movement is quite unlike any other Mendelssohn scherzo; its main theme:

is surprisingly ferocious, and the trio and coda are dark and shadowy, with a menacing *ostinato* phrase in the bass. The *adagio,* though in a major key, is sombre in feeling and achieves something of the seriousness of the slow movement of the B flat Quintet, with less ado. The finale, like the first movement, is frankly orchestral in texture, but has real energy and passion. The exceptionally sad and bitter tone of this work, which may well have resulted from the sudden death of his sister Fanny Hensel, is not to be found in the central movements of the unfinished Quartet that were also written in 1847, and published as Op. 81. The *andante* is a set of variations on a simple and charming theme in E major; they are stricter and more classical in method than usual. The scherzo is as different as possible from that of the F minor Quartet: it is light and delicate, with a touch of wistfulness, and there is a short coda that has no connection with anything else in the movement, yet seems to sum it up perfectly.

CHAPTER X

SYMPHONIES

The Symphony in C minor, Op. 11, was written early in 1824, but, although Mendelssohn was only fifteen, he had previously composed twelve symphonies, and the handling of the orchestra in this work is thoroughly able. The nearest chamber work is the Sextet, Op. 110, which is slightly later; compared with this the Symphony is at the same time more consistent and less enterprising; it has neither the originality of the best nor the vapidity of the worst parts of the Sextet. There is less of the influence of Weber and more of that of Mozart, especially of the G minor Symphony. The slow movement is the maturest part, and its main theme is not unlike that of the *adagio* of the Sextet; like those of the piano quartets, it modulates with more enterprise than the quick movements. The minuet is Mozartian, but the trio suggests the second subject of Weber's *Rübezahl* overture. When the Symphony was performed in 1829 Mendelssohn substituted for the minuet and trio a shortened and beautifully scored orchestral version of the scherzo of the Octet. In both first and last movements there are occasional foretastes of the *Ruy Blas* overture, especially in the second subject of the finale, when a smooth melody is played against short detached chords. But the general impression left by this early Symphony is of ease and technical fluency rather than of individual inspiration.

The 'Reformation' Symphony, published posthumously as Op. 107, was written in 1830 and is thoroughly mature in style, though not completely successful. It was written in celebration of the tercentenary of the Augsburg Protestant Confession, and the first and last movements contain suggestions of a programme connected with the displacement of the Catholic by the Lutheran Church in Germany. The Dresden Amen is introduced, very effectively, at the end of the slow introduction, and again just before the recapitulation of the first movement, and the Lutheran hymn 'Ein' feste Burg' plays an important part in the finale. After a solemn introduction in the major, the first movement opens with the following theme:

which at once suggests the beginning of Haydn's 104th Symphony:

and, quite apart from this resemblance, so much of Mendelssohn's movement, in spite of its indication of tempo, seems really to be slow music in disguise, and the rapid quaver passages achieve fussiness rather than real energy; the pleasant but square-cut second subject is not strong enough for its position. There are, however, impressive things in the movement, especially the un-expectedly quiet opening of the recapitulation after the second appearance of the Dresden Amen. The two central movements are the least pretentious and most successful parts of the work. The second is a tuneful and engaging scherzo with a very happily scored trio; the third is a short and very simple orchestral Song without Words, to which a distinctive flavour is given by the unexpected operatic cliché that reintroduces the main tune, and the reference, in the concluding bars, to the second subject of the first movement. This leads without a break to the introduction to the finale, which is built upon an austerely respectable version of 'Ein' feste Burg,' denuded of such vanities as passing-notes. An effective bridge passage leads to the finale, which is in sonata form and built upon new material. Phrases from the chorale, however, appear in the development, more prominently in the recapitulation and still more emphatically in the coda. Archi-tecturally the movement is interesting and successful, but its thematic invention is undistinguished, particularly the very un-fortunate second subject:

and its aspirations seem to many of us now to be spoilt by a touch of self-consciousness.

From this defect Mendelssohn's next Symphony, published posthumously as Op. 90, is entirely free. Begun during his visit to Italy and finished in Berlin in 1833, it has long been recognized as one of his most wholly successful orchestral works and is known as the 'Italian' Symphony. The first movement has points in common with that of the Octet; there is something of the same exhilaration in its delightfully scored opening, and the form is treated with similar freedom, an entirely new subject being introduced in the development. Especially fine is the passage that leads to the recapitulation, founded on an augmented version of the opening theme, and behind the vivacity of the music there is a breadth that prevents it from falling into the too-comfortable jog-trot into which 6–8 time is liable to lead Mendelssohn. The *andante* is delicately scored and wholly free from sentimentality; it contains passages of unusually bare colouring, and the intro-ductory rhythmic phrase with which it opens is used with both ingenuity and imagination. Mr. Mosco Carner has pointed out in his book *Of Men and Music* how both this movement and the *andante* of Schubert's C major Symphony derive in certain respects from the *allegretto* in Beethoven's seventh Symphony, all three containing suggestions of a procession. The third movement shows Mendelssohn in a more familiar and perhaps more con-ventional mood, but it is beautifully written, and its picturesque trio and coda add a touch of mystery to the generally comfortable and homely atmosphere. The rhythm of the lively main theme of the finale may be an unconscious reminiscence of the tarantella in Weber's piano Sonata in E minor, but the movement as a whole is remarkably original and individual. Rather surprisingly in the tonic minor key throughout, it has great vitality and rhythmic variety, and achieves a strong formal unity with singularly little note-for-note repetition. The composition of this symphony gave Mendelssohn great trouble, and he had intended to revise it before eventually publishing it, but in its present form it remains a most satisfying and spontaneous work.

Ideas for the 'Scottish' Symphony, Op. 56, first occurred to Mendelssohn as early as 1829, but it was not finished till 1842. It is a larger and more ambitious work than the 'Italian' Symphony, less uniformly successful, but very characteristic in both its strength and weakness. The first movement, which is preceded by a short introduction, is remarkable for its orchestral colouring, which is unusually thick and sombre, and the rather square rhythmic shape of the themes here seems curiously suitable for the legendary, narrative atmosphere of the movement. Especially happy points are the modulations at the beginning of the development and coda, the counter-melody played by the cellos against the main theme on its return for the recapitulation and the return of the introduction at the end. Like the three concertos and the E major piano Sonata, this symphony is directed to be played with only the minimum of break between the four movements, and the scherzo brings with it a particularly effective change of colour. It is a delightful movement with a touch of Scottish local colour in its main theme; it is in concise but complete sonata form, with Mendelssohn's usual skill at introducing the recapitulation and an unexpected harmonic progression in the coda:

Vivace non troppo

The *adagio* contains several obvious reminiscences of Beethoven: the main theme looks back to the central section of the *allegretto* of the seventh Symphony and a cadential passage that appears a little later to a similar phrase in the *adagio* of the 'Harp' Quartet. Its sentiment is rich to a fault, though leavened to some extent by very attractive orchestration. The finale is described on the title-page as *Allegro guerriero*, and the complete change of mood in the coda suggests some kind of programme, presumably ending with triumph after battle. The main body of the movement is admirable, with themes of much vitality resourcefully treated; the haunting second subject:

is one of Mendelssohn's best, and the passage in which it dies away before the coda is of very great beauty. After this it must be admitted that the triumphal coda is a disappointment. The thick orchestral texture, which in the first movement was so suited to the generally grey colouring of the music, here seems garish; the melody is commonplace, which is unfortunately emphasized by the direction *maestoso*, and one is tempted to wish that instead of this unconvincing outburst he could have ended quietly, after the manner of the E major piano Sonata or the E flat Quartet, Op. 12, with a reminiscence of the first movement. As it is, he leaves us with the feeling that he is trying here to express a kind of exaltation that was not wholly within his grasp. The 'Scottish' Symphony as a whole leaves a curiously mixed impression, but with all its inequality it is of great interest to the student of Mendelssohn's work for the very complete and varied picture that it gives of his personality.

The orchestral movements of the *Hymn of Praise* will be examined, with the rest of the work, in another chapter.

CHAPTER XI

WORKS FOR A SOLO INSTRUMENT WITH ORCHESTRA

MENDELSSOHN played an important part in the history of the concerto. He was not by temperament a conscious reformer, and it is perhaps significant that the innovations he introduced into the concerto form first appear in a work he himself described as sketchy and hastily written. The first movement of the concerto, as used by Mozart and Beethoven, began with an orchestral *tutti* announcing the main themes of the movement. Mozart, in his piano Concerto, K. 271, and Beethoven, in his fourth and fifth piano Concertos, introduced the soloist for a few bars, before the main business of the *tutti* has begun, but showed no inclination to abolish it. Mendelssohn, in the G minor piano Concerto, Op. 25, not only introduces the soloist early but dispenses entirely with the *tutti*; he also makes the movements lead into each other without a break. In Beethoven's violin Concerto and last two piano Concertos the slow movement leads straight into the finale, but this feature appears in many of the works he wrote at that period, when he seemed to find it curiously difficult to finish a slow movement. But it was only in works of avowedly unconventional design, such as Weber's *Concertstück* for piano and orchestra and Spohr's 'Gesangscene' violin Concerto, that the whole work was played without a break.

The structural unity of the G minor Concerto is further emphasized by the fact that the fanfare-like passage that leads from the first movement to the *andante* reappears between the *andante* and the finale, and that the second subject of the first movement is recalled for a moment in the finale. Architecturally the work is very successful; its musical content is of light weight, with touches of drama in the first movement and of nostalgic sentiment in the second. The finale is cheerful and rather vulgar in its themes, the brilliance of the keyboard writing being often reminiscent of Weber. The traditional cadenza for soloist is, however, abandoned.

The second piano Concerto, in D minor, Op. 40, written five years later, is a work of very similar character, though rather more subdued. The three movements follow each other without a break, but there are no thematic connections between them. The first movement opens impressively, but soon relapses into a conventional and not very effective agitation. The main theme of the *adagio*:

looks back to the familiar phrase from the *larghetto* of Mozart's clarinet Quintet which found so many echoes in the music of Bizet. The finale has the volubility of that of the G minor Concerto, but not its rather engaging pertness.

The remaining works for piano and orchestra are of small importance. The *Capriccio brillant* in B minor, Op. 22, is contemporary with the G minor Concerto and, like several similar works for piano solo, is preceded by a slow introduction in the key of the tonic major. This is strongly influenced by Weber, not only in the material, but in the method of accompanying a sustained melody in the piano part by detached chords, as in the *Concertstück* and the *andante* of the A flat piano Sonata. The main body of the *Capriccio* is suitably vivacious, but is spoilt by a second subject of startling banality:

The *Rondo Brillant*, Op. 29, is harmlessly empty; of the *Serenade*

and Allegro gioioso, Op. 43, written in 1838, the former, in B minor, has considerable charm, but the *Allegro,* although the soloist is frequently instructed to play *con fuoco,* suggests only a very well-behaved and genteel hilarity.

The G minor Concerto still remains an agreeable period piece, but as a whole Mendelssohn's works for piano and orchestra form the most faded group of his instrumental works. On the other hand the violin Concerto in E minor, Op. 64, the last and certainly one of the best of his larger orchestral works, seems hardly to have aged at all. The lateness of its date is worth stressing in view of the prevailing tendency to assume that Mendelssohn's later years represent a steady decline. It has not quite the poetry and imaginativeness of such early works as the Octet and the *Midsummer Night's Dream* and *Hebrides* overtures, but it is full of vitality and does not, like some of Mendelssohn's later works, give the impression that he is trying to recapture something that he has expressed with greater spontaneity in an earlier work. The innovations which he had already introduced into the concerto form are used here on more attractive material; the general atmosphere of the first movement had been anticipated to some extent in that of the string Quartet in the same key, but here finds fuller and more eloquent expression. The opening, with the solo violin singing high up over a simple accompaniment, is extraordinarily effective; equally so are the urgency of the transition theme and the gentle but not over-luscious sentiment of the second subject. The cadenza, discarded in the two piano concertos, here reappears, written by the composer, at the end of the development, and the opening of the recapitulation, at which the main theme is played by the orchestra accompanied by the soloist with figures from the cadenza, is a singularly happy stroke. The moment in the recapitulation at which the second subject appears for the first time in a minor key is remarkably impressive, and, after the passionate coda, the quiet transition to the *andante* is beautifully contrived. This slow movement makes so quick and ready an appeal that it has often been summarily dismissed with contempt resulting from excessive familiarity. It is in a lyrical vein that Mendelssohn has used very frequently, but it is certainly one of the best of its kind, and, in the view of the present writer, its sentiment is strengthened by a feeling of serenity that raises it to a level distinctly higher than that of several of its fellows, such as the slow movements of the piano concertos, the 'Scottish' Symphony and the Trio in C minor. Tovey rightly called attention to the beauty and simplicity of its coda. The finale, introduced by a short bridge-passage of great charm, is the lightest part of the work, but, here again, its value can be seen clearly if it is put beside those of the piano concertos. It is in the same high-spirited mood, but the material is handled with a lighter touch, the virtuosity is less obvious, and there are touches of artistry, such as the introduction of the quiet counter-melody in G major, which never fail to delight. In this work Mendelssohn crystal-lized with complete success his experiments in the handling of the concerto form, and it stands on the same high plane as the 'Italian' Symphony as a comparatively light but highly polished masterpiece, of the kind for which there is always room.

CHAPTER XII

OVERTURES, ETC.

THE earliest overture is that in C for wind instruments (*Ouvertüre für Harmoniemusik*), Op. 24, probably written about 1824. This is not a work of great individuality; the slow introduction is strongly influenced by Mozart and the rest by Weber. But it is thoroughly fluent and ably written, and should be very effective in performance. The so-called 'Trumpet' Overture, published posthumously as Op. 101, dates from 1825, and is a considerably maturer work. The themes are not particularly striking in themselves, but they are treated with real imaginativeness. Its finest passages are at the opening and end of the development, where a phrase from the exposition is put into augmentation and taken through an impressive series of modulations against a shimmering background played by the strings; there is an unmistakable foretaste here of the *Hebrides* and *A Calm Sea and a Prosperous Voyage*.

But, with all its good qualities, this work is outshone by the overture to *A Midsummer Night's Dream* composed in 1826. This is the work of a thoroughly mature composer working at the height of his inspiration. Here the themes are highly individual, and equally remarkable is the skill with which a number of very dissimilar ideas are woven into a highly organized whole. After the magically effective opening chords there is the fairy-like theme in E minor, followed by another of far more ceremonious character in E major, vividly suggestive of Theseus's court. Later comes the gently sentimental theme for the lovers, leading to the very lively portrayal of the rustics, with even a suggestion of Bottom's 'translation.' All these form the material for an admirably balanced movement in sonata form, with a long and imaginative development, and a coda of great beauty in which the fairies have the last word and even spread their spell over Theseus's palace. The orchestration is full of wonderful points, particularly the writing for the woodwind in the development and the quiet drum-roll on the note of the dominant in the final chord, an effect used again by Brahms at the end of the slow movement of his piano Concerto in D minor. Seventeen years later, when Mendelssohn wrote the rest of the incidental music, he was able to show in detail how appropriate are the themes of the overture to the various elements of the play, and it may be doubted whether there has ever been a happier instance of sympathy between music and drama.

The overture inspired by Goethe's twin poems *A Calm Sea* and *A Prosperous Voyage* was written two years later and has something of the same imaginativeness, though it has never been so widely known. Its form is less orthodox than that of the *Midsummer Night's Dream* overture and is guided more by Goethe's words. Beethoven made a choral and orchestral setting of them, and in Mendelssohn's slow introduction, depicting the becalmed sea, there is a surprisingly Beethoven-like stillness and serenity that he often tried very unsuccessfully to convey in later works. There is also a suggestion of Beethoven in the *allegro*, with its combination of surging movement and harmonic breadth; its most prominent theme is very effectively quoted by Elgar in the last but one of the 'Enigma' Variations. The final section, dealing with the triumphant arrival of the ship, is on a somewhat lower level, though it does not produce anything like the jarring effect of the coda of the finale of the 'Scottish' Symphony. After some pompous official greetings the overture ends unexpectedly with a quiet plagal cadence. Tovey has described this as 'a poetic surprise of a high order'; Ernest Walker, on the other hand, saw in it an unwelcome reminder of the presence of the chaplain among those who had assembled on the shore to welcome the vessel.

It was an auspicious moment when Mendelssohn, visiting the Hebrides in August 1829, sketched the opening of what was to be, beyond any doubt, his masterpiece. Its exceptional quality is largely due, as Mr. Hubert Foss has pointed out in the second volume of *The Heritage of Music*, to the fact that it is built, not on the usual symmetrically flowing tune, but on a short rhythmic phrase. This does not often happen in Mendelssohn's work, and two years earlier he had attempted it with peculiarly pedestrian results in the piano Sonata in B flat. In the *Hebrides* overture, however, the theme, for all its simplicity, has a haunting and individual quality, and nothing could be happier or more resourceful than Mendelssohn's treatment of it. Sometimes it is used as a counterpoint to other ideas, and on several occasions it is effectively varied. Mendelssohn had not much sympathy with Schubert's music, but there is a suggestion of Schubert in the spacious imaginativeness of some of the modulations in this work, especially in the wonderful opening of the development which conveys an astonishingly vivid impression of remote distances. The orchestral colouring is highly individual; less persistently thick than the first movement of the 'Scottish' Symphony, but with a greater variety of light and shade than in many of his works. The form is interesting: the outlines of sonata form are preserved, but with great freedom, the recapitulation of the second subject being much shortened and followed by a dramatic coda that rises to a powerful climax and then disappears mysteriously and suddenly. The whole design is singularly convincing, one of the most remarkable features being the restraint that Mendelssohn puts upon the broad and lyrical second subject. Of the overture as a whole it may fairly be said that it combines the best features of his normal style with an added depth of imagination.

The *Melusina* (*Die schöne Melusine*) overture, composed in 1833, is on a lower level of intensity, but it is a very individual and beautifully polished composition for which Mendelssohn himself had a particular affection. The opening bars are worth quoting for their remarkable foretaste of Wagner's Rhine music in *The Ring of the Nibelung* and also for the rhythmic weakness of the third bar, where Mendelssohn's unfortunate tendency to break into block-harmony for a few notes has a rather complacent effect:

But this defect is of small account when set beside the good qualities of this work. Like the *Midsummer Night's Dream* overture, it contains a number of themes of varying character, but the contrasts are not between fairies and humans but between the gentler and stormier aspects of the sea, the former eventually prevailing. As in the *Hebrides* overture, the flexibility of the opening theme contributes to the architectural success of the whole work; it is particularly effective in the development and coda, where it provides a background of quietly rippling movement to passages in which the harmonies move with unusual deliberation. The orchestral colouring is of great beauty throughout, and the serene, thoughtful mood of much of the music is extremely attractive.

The *Ruy Blas* overture, written six years later, is a work of a very different kind. The contrasts here are far more obvious, with all the familiar ingredients of the romantic overture; a grandiose introduction, an agitated main theme and a more lyrical second subject, introduced very effectively against an incisive rhythmic background. Mendelssohn himself had no love for the tragedy by Victor Hugo for which it was written, and there is little in it that can be called tragic at all, but it is written with admirable gusto; there are several moments of vivid dramatic suspense, and, as a piece of vigorous, full-blooded and not too serious melodrama, it is very successful and well deserves its popularity.

The only remaining orchestral works are the exquisitely scored orchestral version of the scherzo of the Octet and two marches. One of these, for wind instruments, was composed for the funeral of Norbert Burgmüller and the other for a festival in honour of the painter Cornelius; neither is of much distinction.

CHAPTER XIII

SONGS, DUETS AND PARTSONGS

A GENERAL idea of the value of Mendelssohn's songs can be obtained by putting them beside their equivalent in the instrumental works, the Songs without Words for piano. Though they are more numerous, a smaller proportion of them sink to the level of the weakest of the piano pieces; on the other hand they do not often rise to the level of the best. They contain much pleasant music, but there is a sameness about them in general, and Mendelssohn did not respond to words with the vivid intuition of Schubert or Schumann.

The first two sets, Opp. 8 and 9, contain four songs and a duet by Mendelssohn's sister Fanny; his own contributions are very varied in value. The first of Op. 8 is a setting of Hölty's *Minnelied*, and a comparison of its opening phrase with that of Brahms's delightful setting of the same words shows only too clearly the rhythmic weakness of Mendelssohn:

An unexpected harmonic touch at the cadence is the only thing that lifts this song from the commonplace; the sombre and reticent *Erntelied* has considerably more character. *Frühlingslied* and *Im Grünen* are fresh and lively, with original touches, such as the opening of the last stanza of the former and the unusual plagal

Mendelssohn

cadence of the latter. But by far the most striking song of this set is *Hexenlied*. Here the 6–8 measure, which can so easily with Mendelssohn become a monotonous amble, is used with real fire, and the music suggests something fiercer and more sinister than the fairy world of *A Midsummer Night's Dream*.

Op. 9 contains nothing as remarkable; the first song, *Frage*, afterwards used in the A minor string Quartet, has a pleasant intimate charm, but *Geständnis*, which, intentionally or not, opens with the same theme, tries to express a more passionate mood with less success. Better than either is *Wartend*, in which the telling simplicity of *Erntelied* recurs in a more vigorous and legendary atmosphere. *Scheidend* is a quietly flowing song of considerable beauty and pathos; its mood and texture look ahead to the more familiar but possibly less distinguished *Auf Flügeln des Gesanges*. *Frühlingsglaube* has a pleasantly exhilarating vivacity, but seems somewhat fussy when compared with Schubert's setting; and it is perhaps significant that at the words 'Nun armes Herze sei nicht bang,' where Schubert writes one of his loveliest phrases, Mendelssohn can produce nothing more eloquent than:

Op. 19a contains *Das erste Veilchen*, in which the phrases are more varied in length and the piano accompaniment richer in melodic interest than usual; the return, towards the end, of the introductory phrase is beautifully contrived. Of the two Heine settings *Neue Liebe* is a brilliantly imaginative song similar in mood to the piano scherzo from Op. 16; *Gruss* is the shortest of all, and one of the very few that might almost be by Schubert; behind its extreme simplicity and homeliness there is great distinction and subtlety of detail. In Op. 34 are two of the songs that achieved the widest popularity, the settings of Heine's *Auf Flügeln des Gesanges* and Goethe's *Suleika* poem, 'Ach um deine

118

feuchten Schwingen.' Of these the first, hackneyed though it has been, still retains great charm; the other is more deeply felt and is in a wistful mood far removed from the curious, ethereal ecstasy of Schubert's setting of these words. In the same set is another Heine song, *Reiselied*, which is powerful and broadly designed, though it has not quite the fire of *Neue Liebe* or *Hexenlied*. The remaining songs in both these sets are pleasant but of less distinction.

Op. 47 contains *Frühlingslied*, to words by Lenau, which has an attractive swinging tune and is the strongest of Mendelssohn's many songs of that title. *Minnelied* and *Der Blumenstrauss* are graceful and neatly written; *Volkslied* is similar in mood to some of the more domestic Songs without Words and has an unassuming simplicity that stops short of sentimentality. The first two of Op. 57, *Altdeutsches Lied* and *Hirtenlied*, are pleasantly friendly and unpretentious, but in the setting of Goethe's other *Suleika* poem, 'Was bedeutet die Bewegung,' what is intended to be ecstatic seems to bounce rather than to soar. At the words 'Ach die wahre Herzenskunde' a quotation from the other *Suleika* song suggests that the two were originally intended to be sung in juxtaposition. The best song in the set is *Venetianisches Gondellied*, the words of which are a translation of Moore's 'When through the Piazzetta.' This is very similar in mood to the gondola songs for piano, and is considerably richer and more interesting than Schumann's surprisingly slight setting of these words.

Op. 57 was the last set of songs to appear in Mendelssohn's life; the posthumous publications vary greatly in date of composition. With one exception, however, the six that were published as Op. 71 were written during his last years. The three latest, written in 1847, are all of interest: *An die Entfernte* has remarkable neatness and charm, and in *Auf der Wanderschaft* there is, exceptionally, a touch of Schubert, especially in the final stanza. Finer than either is *Nachtlied*, which achieves a quiet solemnity to which

Mendelssohn often tried to attain with far less success; in the final stanza there is a most eloquent and moving climax. *Schilflied*, written in 1842, is in the more familiar gondola song manner, expressed with great charm and delicacy. The first of Op. 86, *Es lausche das Laub*, was written as early as 1826; it is an interesting though not entirely convincing song, beginning in the major and ending in the minor. There is a difference of text between the English and German editions, the former containing, towards the end, a fine passage that may well have been inserted by Mendelssohn at a later date. The third song of the set, *Die Liebende schreibt*, to words by Goethe, is one of Mendelssohn's best—it was composed in 1831. Here, as in *Das erste Veilchen*, the phraseology is more varied than usual, especially at the words 'Die einzige, dann fang ich an zu weinen.' A comparison with Brahms's setting is of interest; Brahms, usually so much more flexible and varied in his rhythms than Mendelssohn, here follows the metre of the poem with a rather self-conscious persistence. On the other hand, in the next song of the set Mendelssohn's treatment of Heine's *Allnächtlich im Traume* is ineffective beside the inspired simplicity of Schumann's setting. *Der Mond* is pleasantly rich, though free from sentimentality; *Altdeutsches Frühlingslied*, Mendelssohn's last composition, has attractive ideas, but there is a sketchiness about it that suggests exhaustion.

The first of Op. 99, a setting of Goethe's *Erster Verlust*, is a sincere and carefully wrought song, but it cannot bear comparison with the effortless simplicity and pathos of the setting of these words composed by Schubert at the age of sixteen. Two others in this set, *Die Sterne schau'n in stiller Nacht* and *Es weiss und rät es doch Keiner*, have a greater diversity of mood than is usual in the songs; apart from this neither is of special interest. *Das Schifflein* has attractive moments, but the eternally ambling sextuple time makes it monotonous. On the other hand in *Jagdlied*, the third song of Op. 84, the same 6–8 measure is handled far more skilfully, with an attractive variety of phrase-lengths. This set also contains *Da lieg' ich unter den Bäumen,* another song that begins in the major and ends in the minor. The songs published with-out opus numbers include two settings of Byron, *There be none of beauty's daughters* and *Sun of the sleepless,* of which the latter is the more distinguished, and two of Eichendorff, *Das Waldschloss* and *Pagenlied,* which are both attractive, especially the former. The setting of Moore's *The Garland* is charming and that of Schiller's *Des Mädchens Klage,* more ambitious than Schubert's, is of considerable interest; its restless atmosphere and surging accompaniment are prophetic of Brahms.

The six duets with piano accompaniment, Op. 63, are all of pleasant quality. For the most part the two voices move together, but in *Herbstlied,* which is on the whole the most interesting of them, the second part shows more independence. *Abschiedslied der Zugvögel* has great delicacy and charm, *Volkslied*—alias 'O wert thou in the cauld blast' (Burns)—has an appealing simplicity, and the opening theme of *Gruss,* quoted elsewhere, is highly characteristic. *Maiglöckchen und die Blümelein* is the most vivacious, and the texture of the piano accompaniment is similar to the slightly later Song without Words in A from the eighth book. Of the three duets, Op. 77, the most striking is the second, *Das Aehrenfeld,* written in 1847; the change to the sombre mood of the last lines is all the more impressive for the lightness of touch with which it is carried out. The three *Volkslieder* are not of particular interest; the best is the plaintive 'Wie kann ich froh und lustig sein?'

The unaccompanied partsongs for mixed voices are more numerous than the duets, but they are too similar in general character to need much detailed description. They are always neatly written and very pleasant to hear, but of all Mendelssohn's works they reflect most clearly the conventionally well-mannered social background against which he spent so much of his time, and they are liable to cloy in too large quantities. Of the first set, Op. 41, *Mailied* and *Auf dem See* have more variety of texture than the rest, especially the latter, which is one of the best. From Op. 48 *Lerchengesang* contains some lively and attractive contra-puntal writing; the opening section of *Herbstlied* is of considerable beauty, which unfortunately emphasizes the far less distinguished quality of the latter part. *Abschied vom Wald*, from Op. 59, is a characteristic example of the type of partsong that had so profound an influence on some of the contributors to *Hymns Ancient and Modern*; its sentiment may seem over-sweet, but to dismiss it on that account as insincere would be unfair. *Die Nachtigall*, more contrapuntal than most, is beautifully written and *Jagdlied* has some very effective moments, especially the return of the opening theme just before the end. Op. 88 contains *Hirtenlied*, which also exists as a solo song, and the pleasantly vivacious *Die Wald-vöglein*. Of the four partsongs of Op. 100 the most attractive is the fresh and delicate *Frühlingslied*. Of the male-voice partsongs the more serious are inclined to be stodgy, apart from the charming *Wasserfahrt* from Op. 50, but the lighter songs sometimes show a pleasant vein of comedy not often to be found in Mendelssohn; *Türkisches Schenkenlied, Liebe und Wein* and *Zigeunerlied* are amusing examples. Op. 120 contains a spirited setting of a translation of Scott's 'Waken, Lords and Ladies gay.'

CHAPTER XIV

ORATORIOS

THE development of the oratorio during the eighteenth century was curiously chequered. Those of Handel were a kind of extension of his stage works; many of them have a strong narrative interest, and the problems of choral counterpoint often resulted in a powerful dramatic tension that is seldom to be found in the operas. Still less does it appear in the oratorios of Handel's successors. The greatness of Haydn's *Creation* is of a very different kind, Beethoven's *Christus am Oelberge* was an early by-product and Spohr's musical personality was far too amiable for him to be able to deal adequately with subjects as formidable as *The Last Judgment* or *The Fall of Babylon*. Mendelssohn was an earnest student of the works of both J. S. Bach and Handel, and in his oratorios we can see him clearly trying to emulate the introspective profundity of the one and the dramatic force of the other.

In *St. Paul* the dramatic element is less prominent than in *Elijah*, and the use of chorales suggests at least the methods of Bach. In some ways this is unfortunate; the treatment of chorales is one of the things in which Bach has set so supremely high a standard that it is difficult to judge any later attempts in the same field without unconscious comparisons. But of the chorales in *St. Paul* it can be said generally that their treatment, if not particularly distinguished, is adequate and dignified, and that there are no jarring lapses such as the unfortunate harmonization of 'Nun danket' in the *Hymn of Praise*. The overture opens with a slow introduction based upon 'Wachet auf'; this leads to a fugal movement which, as so often in Mendelssohn, gradually increases in speed and intensity. The first phrase of the chorale appears from time to time, and eventually a considerable part of it is used in the coda. It is a fine and solidly built movement, though it has not quite the sustained excitement of others of its type, such as the E minor Fugue from Op. 35, the first movement of the A major organ Sonata or the overture to *Elijah*; this may perhaps be due to the rather pompous effect of the transformation of the chorale phrases to triple time.

The dotted-note figure that introduces the first chorus at once suggests Handel; the music is massive and effectively written, but it must be admitted that as a setting of the words 'Lord, Thou alone art God, and Thine are the Heavens, the earth, and the mighty waters. The Heathen furiously rage, Lord, against Thee, and Thy Christ. Now behold, lest our foes prevail, Lord, grant to Thy servants all strength and joyfulness,' it is somewhat stolid and lacking in urgency; particularly the phrase:

The Hea then fu-rious-ly rage, Lord, a - gainst Thee and Thy Christ

After the chorale that follows, however, everything becomes considerably more vital, and in the chorus 'Now this man ceaseth not' we are reminded of Handel, not by any individual feature in the music, but by its remarkable fire and energy. The musical invention is here far more vigorous, and the periodic recurrences of the opening trumpet-call make not only for formal unity, but also for a strong sense of dramatic tension; the abrupt concluding bars are particularly effective. The recitative for Stephen that follows is frankly operatic in character, and the soprano solo 'Jerusalem, thou that slayest the prophets' has a lyric flow that owes much to Italy—more perhaps than the composer imagined. Here again the music hardly suggests the sorrowful reproach of the words, but it has considerable beauty, and the treatment of the opening phrase gives it a distinction not always to be found in solos of this kind. The chorus 'Stone him to death,' though vigorous, relies too much on rhythmic reiteration to be quite convincing and has not the power and spaciousness of 'Now this man ceaseth not'; its most effective feature is the hammering sequential passage near the end at the words 'He blasphemes God, and who does so shall surely perish.' On the other hand 'Happy and blest are they' is a choral and orchestral lyric of great charm and has a very attractive idyllic serenity.

The next two movements are on a lower level; Saul's solo 'Consume them all, Lord Sabaoth' leaves an impression of rather ineffectual bluster, largely owing to the square and pedestrian rhythm of the vocal part, and the arioso 'But the Lord is mindful of his own' is weakly sentimental, its most attractive phrase being a misplaced reminiscence of the slow movement of Beethoven's violin Concerto. With the conversion of Saul, however, the interest revives. The setting of 'Saul, why persecutest thou Me' for women's voices supported by wind instruments is highly effective, and the chorus that follows, 'Arise, shine,' is one of the most vital in the oratorio. It opens with a long orchestral *crescendo* which is admirably built up; its only weak moment comes at the climax, where, as on other occasions, Mendelssohn holds up the rhythm by breaking into block harmony for two bars. The chorus itself is long and vigorous, with an elaborate fugal section in the middle; the final pages have an exultant breadth which considerably exceeds that of the rather similar conclusion of 'Be not afraid' from *Elijah*. The scoring of the final chords, for wind only, is noteworthy as being a kind of apotheosis of the orchestral accompaniment to 'Saul, why persecutest thou Me.' A harmonization of 'Wachet auf' punctuated simply but effectively by fanfares on the trumpets and horns is followed by the bass solo 'O Lord, have mercy.' This is the finest solo in the work; opening with a very expressive phrase:

played by oboe and bassoon in octaves, it has true dignity and pathos, the only possible criticism being that, after the more dramatic central section the return of the first theme might have been more prolonged. A short recitative, in which the voice of the Lord is again accompanied by wind instruments, leads to one of the most unexpected movements of the oratorio. The bass solo sings 'I praise Thee, O Lord my God, with all my heart for ever more; for great is Thy mercy towards me and Thou hast delivered my soul from the lowest Hell,' to which the chorus replies: 'The Lord, He is good: He shall dry your tears and heal your sorrows, for His word shall not decay.' All this is set to a gently flowing 6–8 rhythm in A minor; it is entirely free from squareness, and towards the end the chorus is developed with considerable breadth, but as a setting of these words it is surprisingly subdued. The following recitative returns to a more dramatic style, and leads eventually to the chorus 'O great is the depth,' the opening theme of which is very effectively anticipated. This returns to the dignified, ceremonial mood of the opening chorus, but it has more vitality and urgency, especially in the long and increasingly animated fugal setting of the words 'Sing His glory for evermore,' after which the return of the first theme of the chorus brings the first part of *St. Paul* to an impressive end.

In the second part there is less action and the musical interest flags more frequently. There is a fine spaciousness in the setting of 'The Nations now are the Lord's' with which it opens; this leads to a fugal chorus, 'For all the Gentiles come before Thee,' solidly built and perhaps over-long but thoroughly workmanlike and effective, especially in the final pages, where the two main themes are worked simultaneously. Perhaps as a reaction from the rather impersonal style of this chorus, the duet 'Now we are ambassadors' and the chorus 'How lovely are the messengers' are in Mendelssohn's more familiar lyrical manner; the amiably lilting rhythm and smooth, flowing texture of the latter won it immediate popularity, and there are points of polished workmanship that lift it from the level of the commonplace. The arioso 'I will sing of Thy great mercies' is not of great interest, but after it the short chorus 'Thus saith the Lord' introduces a more vital atmosphere. The next chorus, 'Is this he?,' opens in a rhythm that comes dangerously near to jauntiness, but in its later stages, after the introduction of the phrase

this impression is greatly diminished by the increase of contrapuntal tension, and the chorale setting that follows, with its flowing accompaniment, is undoubtedly the most beautiful in the work. After a mildly sermonizing duet for Paul and Barnabas, 'For so hath the Lord Himself commanded,' the healing of the lame man by Paul is depicted in a manner that seems hardly to justify the excitement of the heathen's 'The gods themselves have descended,' which is portrayed with considerable vividness. In 'O be gracious, ye immortals' Mendelssohn, as in the familiar 'Baal, we cry to thee' chorus from *Elijah*, employs the device of frequent repetition of a single short phrase, presumably in order to suggest an atmosphere of unenlightened paganism. Here, however, it is done far more sympathetically than in the later chorus; indeed the music, with its delightful and picturesquely scored orchestral accompaniment, has so much charm that we may almost suspect him of a secret sympathy for the heathen. A recitative and arioso for bass leads to the chorus 'But our God abideth in Heaven,' an impressively austere and contrapuntal movement built round a chorale, and very far removed from the popular conception of Mendelssohn's personality. The next chorus, 'This is Jehovah's temple,' returns to the rather fussy indignation of 'Stone him to death,' a reminiscence of which occurs at the end. Of the remaining movements the best is the short chorus 'See what love hath the Father bestowed,' the quiet contrapuntal flow of which looks forward to the still more successful 'He that shall endure to the end' from *Elijah*. The tenor solo 'Be thou faithful unto death' is in a mood that is expressed less pretentiously but with greater charm in some of the Songs without Words, and the final chorus, 'Bless thou the Lord, O my soul,' is solidly built but pedestrian in its general effect. Considered as a whole, *St. Paul* does not rise to the level of the best things in *Elijah*, nor sink to that of the weakest. It is an eminently serious and sincere work, worthy at least of respect and sometimes of more.

The *Hymn of Praise*, described by its composer as a 'symphony-cantata,' is built on a plan similar to that of Beethoven's ninth Symphony, three instrumental movements being followed by an extended choral finale. The proportions are, however, entirely different, Mendelssohn's instrumental movements being on a far smaller scale than those of Beethoven. For many years it was one of the most popular of Mendelssohn's works; now, generally speaking, it seems one of the most faded—considerably more so than *St. Paul*. The first movement is handicapped by the complacently pompous opening theme: [1]

which is effective in the ceremonious introduction, but has not enough character to be suitable for the amount of development that it afterwards receives. The movement as a whole leaves the impression of an efficient but slightly mechanical brightness; the second subject would be more effective if Beethoven had not already used practically the same idea with considerably more distinction in the first movement of the piano Sonata in B flat, Op. 22. The *allegretto* that follows is, in its first and third sections, far more spontaneous; it is a pleasant Gondola Song

[1] At an early performance of the work, the trombonist attempted to enliven it by introducing a turn after the first beat of the second bar; Mendelssohn, to his credit, was amused.

spoilt only by the misguided ingenuity that impelled Mendelssohn
to base the central portion on the opening theme of the work.
The *adagio* is not unlike that of the 'Scottish' Symphony, but it is
less attractive both thematically and orchestrally, with the result
that its sentiment seems stodgy and rather oppressive. The introduction to the first chorus makes effective use of the opening theme
of the work and of a rhythmic figure from the *adagio*, but the
chorus itself is not of great interest; the central section, to the
words 'And let all flesh magnify His might and His glory,' has
more character than the rest. Neither the soprano solo with
chorus, 'Praise thou the Lord, O my spirit,' nor the tenor solo,
'He counteth all your sorrows,' call for much comment, but the
chorus 'All ye that cried unto the Lord' has some pleasantly
flowing part-writing. In the duet with chorus, 'I waited for the
Lord,' there is some neat and charming workmanship, especially
towards the end, but the melody seems a little too comfortable to
be appropriate. A comparison between this and the rather
similar Song without Words in B flat from the seventh book
is of some interest. The piano piece, which goes at a livelier
pace, does not attempt to be more than pleasant drawing-room
music, which it achieves with some success; 'I waited for the
Lord' aims higher, but falls lower. The next movement contains by far the most interesting music in the work. There is
considerable pathos in the opening of the tenor solo 'The sorrows
of death':

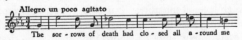

Allegro un poco agitato

The sor - rows of death had clo - sed all a - round me

and in the setting of the dialogue with the watchman that follows,
Mendelssohn, inspired, it is said, by a sleepless night, conveys a
remarkable atmosphere of dramatic suspense. The entry of the
soprano solo with the words 'The night is departing' is thrilling;
unfortunately the succeeding chorus, though it tries hard to be
impressive, has something of the same sense of anticlimax as the

final section of the 'Scottish' Symphony. The setting of the familiar chorale 'Nun danket' begins well, but the second stanza, with its elaborate orchestral accompaniment, is spoilt by a strange and disconcerting harmonic miscalculation:

where, as Hadow pointed out in *Studies in Modern Music*, 'the last chord is simply out of balance.' The duet 'My song shall be always of Thy mercy' is flowing and lyrical, with an engagingly demure setting of the words 'I wander in night and foulest darkness and mine enemies threatening around.' After this the work ends, as might be expected, with a pompously energetic semi-fugal chorus, concluded by a reminiscence of the opening theme.

To turn from this work to *Elijah* is to feel at once a complete change of atmosphere. The *Hymn of Praise* was written for an official function and only occasionally does it rise above the level of a *pièce de circonstance*. In *Elijah*, with all its inequality, it is obvious that Mendelssohn was genuinely stirred by the dramatic power of the story, which often roused him to write at an unusually high level of intensity. It is clear from his correspondence with Schubring that he was anxious for a libretto which could provide every opportunity for drama, and there is no doubt that, in the words of Tovey, he possessed 'the capacity for thrilling dramatic moments.' What he lacked, however, was the sustained intensity and staying power of such composers as Verdi and Wagner, and the less satisfactory features in *Elijah* are where there seems to be an imperfect collaboration between his lyrical and dramatic instincts. At first, however, there is no trace of this;

Elijah's sombre recitative prophesying the drought makes a remarkably original and impressive opening to the oratorio. Particularly effective is the series of diminished fifths that recurs on several later occasions, almost as a kind of 'curse motive.' This is followed at once by the overture, the last and perhaps the finest of the movements in which Mendelssohn uses a fugal texture as a means of building up a gradually increasing tension. From time to time the wind recall the rhythm of the last words of the recitative 'Ich sage es denn,' the effect of which is lost in the English version 'but according to my word.' Eventually the overture leads straight into the first chorus, 'Help, Lord,' which has something of the same spaciousness as the opening chorus of *St. Paul*, but far greater urgency and far more thematic distinction. After its massive introductory phrases a freely fugal texture once more leads to a climax, and a short recitative of considerable pathos leads to the duet with chorus, 'Lord, bow Thine ear to our prayer.' This is lyrical in mood, but a curiously haunting character is given to it by the chorus's frequent reiterations of the opening words, to the same musical phrase on different degrees of the scale. The lyricism of Obadiah's 'If with all your hearts' is of a more luxuriant, Italianate kind; its orchestral accompaniment is beautifully scored, and, as so often, the return of the main tune is very neatly worked. The next chorus, 'Yet doth the Lord see it not,' opens with great power, the sinister diminished fifths of the opening recitative being very effectively introduced to the words 'His curse hath fallen down upon us'; it culminates in a chorale, the melody of which, like that of the others in *Elijah*, is Mendelssohn's own. The concluding section, in C major, though richly sonorous, is less interesting. The double quartet 'For He shall give His angels,' placid rather than angelic, is written with a keen sense of choral colour, and is charming to hear. It is followed by what Tovey described as 'the all too lifelike tiresomeness of the widow,' a passage in which Mendelssohn seems to be veering rather uneasily towards the world of opera; its most effective moment is the reminiscence, to the words 'Thou shalt love the Lord thy God,' of Elijah's first recitative. Far more successful is the chorus 'Blessed are the men who fear Him,' which is very similar in atmosphere to 'Happy and blest are they' from *St. Paul*; flowing vocal phrases are treated contra-puntally against a delightful murmuring background in which Mendelssohn's orchestral sense is at its finest.

At this early stage in the oratorio we already have a general idea of its strength and weakness. The finest work is un-doubtedly in the choruses, which range from massive energy to idyllic serenity; the episode of the healing of the widow's son calls for a more vivid portrayal of the miraculous than was at Mendelssohn's command, and the lyricism of such things as 'If with all your hearts' and 'He shall give His angels,' with all its charm, is a little too comfortable and mellifluous for the general feeling of the work. The remainder of the first part maintains on the whole a remarkably high level and contains some of the most dramatic music that Mendelssohn ever wrote. Elijah, re-turning after three years' absence, prophesies an end to the drought and the music recalls, in more genial colours, his opening recitative. After a short dialogue with Ahab, he issues his challenge to the priests of Baal to call on their god to show his superiority. The gradually increasing tension of this scene is built up with re-markable power. The first chorus of the priests opens with a short melodic phrase that is repeated many times and eventually worked canonically; its second section is more animated but equally primitive melodically. The next chorus is far more agitated and the third rushes along in 6–8 time, which is here employed with real fire. After some very effective dramatic pauses comes Elijah's solo 'Lord God of Abraham'; this is introduced by an impressive modulation and avoids the sanctimoniousness into which Men-delssohn might easily have fallen. It has a true breadth and dignity that reaches its climax with the return of the main melody in D flat. Equally effective is the reminiscence, after the final plagal cadence, of the opening phrase, which is recalled also at the end of the quiet chorale-like quartet 'Cast thy burden upon the Lord' that follows. The chorus 'The fire descends from Heaven' is vividly exciting, and concludes very impressively with a chorale. The recitative in which Elijah orders the destruction of the prophets of Baal is rather conventionally theatrical, but his solo 'Is not His word like a fire?' is undoubtedly the finest in the oratorio. Its hammering energy is worthy of the central section of 'But who shall abide?' from *Messiah*, and it achieves very successfully what Mendelssohn had aimed at with far less certainty in 'Consume them all' from *St. Paul*. The contralto solo 'Woe unto them' is less striking, but has a moment of curiously Schubertian pathos towards the end when the music goes quietly into the key of the tonic major. The scene in which Elijah prays for rain is unequal in quality; its opening is one of the weakest and most sentimental passages in the work, but the solo for the boy who is sent up to look for the first cloud brings a breath of air into the music, and there is a striking chain of modulations leading to the chorus 'Thanks be to God.' This is a broad and exultant movement, with a wide range of key and some harmonic clashes such as

which appear to have caused some heart-searchings at early rehearsals. The violin figure suggested by the words 'The waters gather, they rush along' has great impetus, which culminates in the very effective descending scale just before the last return of the main theme.

The second part of *Elijah*, like that of *St. Paul*, is more uneven in quality than the first. Haunted, perhaps, by memories of Bach's St. Matthew Passion, Mendelssohn opens it with a woman's solo in B minor and in slow 3–8 time, 'Hear ye, Israel.'

It is written, however, for soprano, not contralto, and is in two sections, the second being in a quicker tempo and in the major key. Both are good; the first has considerable pathos and the second recalls the vigour of the march movement from the C minor organ Sonata with an added sense of urgency. Maria Caradori-Allan's opinion that it was 'not a lady's song' is probably a back-handed testimony to its vitality. For the next chorus, 'Be not afraid,' the key changes without any intervening steps, from B to G; the modulation is in itself very effective, but the chorus is square and pedestrian. The frequent reiterations of the

rhythm seem so much more at home in the burlesque pomposity of the entrance of the Peers in Sullivan's *Iolanthe*. As so often, the most effective moment is the return to the main theme. For the scene with Jezebel Mendelssohn returns to the quasi-operatic style of the episode of the healing of the widow's son, but with greater success and more vivid sense of drama. It culminates with the chorus 'Woe to him,' which far excels its equivalent in *St. Paul*, 'Stone him to death,' owing to its greater rhythmic variety; the final *diminuendo* is particularly impressive. The bass solo that follows again suggests a comparison with *St. Paul*, but here the balance favours the earlier work. Elijah's 'It is enough' has a broad and attractive melody and never fails in its effect, but it has not quite the distinction and pathos of 'O Lord, have mercy,' which it so resembles in its general plan. Its finest moment is in the final section, where the overlapping phrases for voice and cello suggest beautifully the gradual exhaustion of Elijah. To comfort him, three angels sing the slight but charming trio, 'Lift thine eyes,' which is followed by 'He watching over Israel.' This is a chorus of singular beauty and poetry, in a serenely unsentimental mood; the part-writing is full of subtle and inobtrusive artistry. A rather perfunctory recitative is followed by the contralto solo

'O rest in the Lord,' which has perhaps been more extravagantly praised and blamed than anything else in the work. The truth probably lies somewhere between the two extremes; it makes a ready appeal and contains some neat and fluent writing, but its atmosphere, compared with that of the preceding chorus, sounds undeniably parochial, and, as Tovey pointed out, its dramatic appropriateness is seriously impaired by the fact that, for reasons of economy, it is usually sung by Jezebel. The chorus that follows, 'He that shall endure to the end,' has never achieved so wide a popularity, but it is of far more distinguished quality; behind its quiet contrapuntal flow is a deeply contemplative beauty almost worthy of Bach. After a short recitative which looks back very effectively to the opening chorus, the oratorio reaches its most dramatic point in the chorus 'Behold, the Lord passed by.' The music depicting the wind, the earthquake and the fire has vigour, urgency and an admirably devised scheme of modulations carried out with unusual breadth, and for the still, small voice Mendelssohn was able to revert to something more like his normal manner without loss of dignity, maintaining an atmosphere of strong but gentle serenity. After this the interest of the oratorio generally declines. The chorus 'Holy, holy is God the Lord' is dignified and sonorous, but the thematic material is undistinguished. Elijah's arioso 'For the mountains shall depart' has a pleasant lyrical flow, but its rhythm seems to hover uneasily between that of a barcarolle and a waltz, and as the last song of the most important character in the story it is lacking in significance. For the chorus describing Elijah's ascent to heaven the interest revives, especially at the passage describing the chariot of fire and the horses, which is introduced by a very effective modulation. The tenor solo 'Then shall the righteous' is more conventional; neither of the two remaining choruses, 'But the Lord from the north hath raised one' and 'And then shall your light,' is of great interest, but they are separated by the quartet 'O come, everyone that thirsteth,' a movement of great freshness and charm. Just before the end of the final chorus Mendelssohn, intentionally or otherwise, recalls the diminished fifths of the opening recitative.

For many years *Elijah* was regarded, in England at least, as Mendelssohn's masterpiece, and equal in merit to the oratorios of Handel. Occasionally, as in 'Is not His word like a fire?' and in some of the choruses, Mendelssohn approaches the dramatic fire and inspired obviousness of Handel, but in general his approach to biblical words was more introspective and less spontaneous. It is not fair to judge *Elijah* either by Handelian standards or by those of Mendelssohn's own best secular works, but, if it is taken on its own merits, there is much in it that still entitles it to be regarded as a fine and lovable work.

Compared with *St. Paul* it is less homogeneous and, apart from the overture, it contains fewer examples of the contrapuntal skill that is now regarded as one of the most attractive features of Mendelssohn's style, though earlier critics such as Grove and H. F. Chorley seemed to have thought it a kind of youthful indiscretion that he outgrew in maturity. But there is no doubt that the drama of *Elijah* stirred him to a higher degree of intensity than is ever found in *St. Paul.* Of the quieter portions the best are distinguished by an idyllic serenity that has no suggestion of ecclesiasticism about it; apart from 'He that shall endure to the end' the most devotional parts of the work are the least distinguished. Bearing this in mind it is interesting to speculate on the probable character of the unfinished oratorio *Christus*, of which only a few numbers survive. The use of traditional chorales suggests that, as might be expected from the nature of the subject, Mendelssohn wanted to return to the more contemplative atmosphere of *St. Paul.* There is an attractive spaciousness in the chorus 'There shall a star from Jacob come forth,' and at the opening of 'Crucify Him' the gradual ascent has considerable dramatic power. But the general impression of this torso is somewhat colourless; Mendelssohn's idiom had not the universality of that of J. S. Bach, which could express with equal success the tensest drama and the deepest devotion. There are signs in *Christus* that his desire to approach the subject in a devout and restrained manner might have resulted in a lack of real musical vitality.

CHAPTER XV

OTHER CHORAL WORKS

APART from the oratorios the most interesting choral work is undoubtedly the setting of Goethe's *Die erste Walpurgisnacht*. It is not all equally good, but the finest things in it are a notable expansion of a mood that appeared on a smaller scale in the songs *Hexenlied* and *Neue Liebe*, dealing with the more formidable aspects of fairyland. For the overture Mendelssohn, influenced perhaps by Haydn's *The Seasons*, wrote a stormy movement entitled *Das schlechte Wetter* which leads to a quieter passage depicting the approach of spring and eventually leading into the first chorus. The first part is vigorous and resourceful, its main theme having a close resemblance to the opening of the 'Scottish' Symphony; the second makes much use of a figure which, as Fuller-Maitland pointed out many years ago, has a curious foretaste of the first movement of Brahms's second Symphony:

Allegro vivace non troppo

The opening chorus, in which the pagans and Druids greet the approach of May, opens freshly and cheerfully, but grows more menacing towards the end, at the mention of sacrificial fires. They are then warned by an old woman of the punishments with which they will be afflicted if they are caught by Christians. This is followed by a solo for the Druid priest, not of great interest in itself, but effectively punctuated by the chorus. After an animated and mildly conspiratorial chorus, a Druid sentinel remarks, in the words of W. Bartholomew's translation:

> Should our Christian foes assail us,
> Aid a scheme that may avail us!
> Feigning demons, whom they fable,
> We will scare the bigot rabble.

This leads to the chorus 'Kommt mit Zacken,' which is by far the finest part of the work, and one of the most powerful things that Mendelssohn ever wrote. It begins in a stealthy, march-like rhythm, with an increasingly elaborate orchestral accompaniment, the writing for the woodwind being particularly picturesque; eventually a brilliantly effective modulation introduces a long and vigorous movement in rapid 6-8 time, which is from time to time broken by two bars of duple rhythm:

When this has reached its climax the priest introduces a more solemn note, and the music declines considerably in vitality. The agitated scattering of the Christians is vividly portrayed, but the work ends in a rather conventionally pompous mood with a final appearance and amplification of the priest's music. Among Mendelssohn's choral works *Die erste Walpurgisnacht* has features of outstanding interest; apart from the great merit of much of the music, it throws important light on the probable strength and weakness of a full-sized operatic venture. The finest movement is undoubtedly the chorus of malignant spirits; the fact that these in reality are merely pagans in disguise is immaterial. But for the individuals, the priest, the old woman and the sentinels, the music, though not inappropriate, is less distinctive and suggests that, however admirable its music might be, a Mendelssohn opera would have been unlikely to contain any unforgettable pieces of musical characterization.

Next in order of magnitude is *Lauda Sion*, a work of very different character. It is Mendelssohn's largest setting of Latin words, and, though it contains nothing outstanding in the way of musical invention, its spacious and polished technique deserves admiration. In the opening section the harmonies move with a Beethoven-like breadth and deliberation, and the first entry of the chorus is admirably timed. The orchestral accompaniments of the quartet 'In hac mensa novi regis' and the treble solo 'Caro cibus, sanguis portus' are beautifully scored, especially the latter, with its very delicate colouring, and there is a touch of unwonted austerity in the chorus 'Docti sacris institutis.' The weakness of the work is that Mendelssohn's very close adherence to the metre of the short lines of the Latin hymn is apt to lead to the reiteration of rather pedestrian rhythms such as:

or:

which his contrapuntal skill can palliate but not completely cover. A comparison with the *Stabat Mater* of either Palestrina or Verdi shows this at once. It is least evident in the massive chorus 'Sumit unus, sumunt mille'; the serene final movement, 'Bone Pastor,' seems at the same time to look back to the Beethoven of the Mass in C and forward to certain things in the Brahms Requiem.

The five accompanied settings of Psalms vary considerably in value. The earliest, Op. 31, composed in 1830, is a setting of Psalm CXV, 'Not unto us, O Lord'; the first movement is in Mendelssohn's most vigorous and contrapuntal vein, and the occasional incursions into block harmony do not, as so often, hold up the flow of the music but come with a kind of Handelian inevitability. The duet 'House of Israel' is in the familiar flowing 6–8 rhythm, with some simple but effective part-writing;

the bass solo 'The Lord shall increase you' has dignity and some happy points of thematic treatment. A broad and simple unaccompanied passage leads to a gently elegiac final section. The settings of Psalm XLII, Op. 42, and Psalm XCV, Op. 46, are more ambitious and less successful. The first chorus of Op. 42 opens in a rhythm that comes dangerously near that of a slow waltz, though this feeling is lessened as the texture grows more elaborate. The treble solo 'For my soul thirsteth for God' with oboe *obbligato* is far less pretentious but has a gentle and appealing pathos. The rest of the work is solid and workmanlike but not of great interest; there are fine moments in the quintet with treble solo and the long final chorus, but neither seems completely to leave the ground.

The setting of the Psalm XCV, Op. 46, appears to have caused Mendelssohn some indecision and is a somewhat puzzling composition. It begins with a setting of the sixth verse, 'O come, let us worship and fall down and kneel before the Lord our maker'; the first two verses follow, introduced by a very effective change from E flat to C major; the music is lively and exhilarating, the frequently recurring § ♩. ♪♩ ♩. rhythm being much more suitable to the German 'Kommet herzu' than to the English 'Come, let us sing.' An impressive canonic section follows, to 'For He is a great God, and a great King above all gods.' The next movement is a lyrical duet which, incidentally, deals with the sixth verse again; then there is a chorus beginning with 'The sea is His and He made it,' which contains references to the theme of the opening movement. It leads straight into another chorus which covers the last four verses of the Psalm; this is for the most part quiet and elegiac in tone, though there are two surprisingly operatic outbursts for 'Unto whom I sware in My wrath, that they should not enter into My rest.' Here the work originally ended, but after the first performance in 1839 Mendelssohn added another chorus in which the opening theme of the Psalm is again used. This makes a more satisfactory end, but, on the other hand, it is very similar in mood to some of the earlier movements, it deals with verses that have been already set and it results in excessive length. The work contains some fine music and the two operatic passages already mentioned are interesting as attempts at an unusually dramatic treatment of biblical words, but it cannot be regarded as a very satisfactory whole.

The most impressive of these accompanied Psalm settings is undoubtedly that of Psalm CXIV, 'When Israel out of Egypt came,' which deserves to be far more widely known. The opening section is remarkable for its deliberate but never flagging move-ment, which produces a broad spaciousness by no means common in Mendelssohn. In the section beginning 'The sea saw and fled' the varying degrees of agitation are presented with great skill and power; after the solemn setting of 'What ailed thee, thou sea, that thou fleddest' the modulation to C major for 'At the Lord's coming ye trembled' is thrilling; the phrase

Allegro maestoso vivace

is a singularly appropriate setting for 'Who turned the hard rock into standing water.' In the final section, in which material from the opening section recurs, Mendelssohn is, again, unusual in con-veying a feeling of exultation that so often seems to be just beyond his grasp. The splendid quality of this work can at once be felt if it is put beside the setting of Psalm XCVIII that Mendelssohn composed for the New Year festivities in Berlin for 1844; here the usual technical efficiency cannot disguise a poverty of idea, and the music never rises above an air of perfunctory and official rejoicing.

Of the remaining works for chorus and orchestra the largest is *Tu es Petrus*, composed in 1827 for his sister's birthday. This is a massive and broadly designed composition, rather impersonal in idiom, but showing a command of polyphonic technique astonishing in a composer of eighteen. The two

remaining works are amiable but not of great importance. *Verleih'
uns Frieden*, written in 1831, anticipates in its accompaniment the
opening theme of the slightly later *Melusina* overture. The
Hymn for alto solo, chorus and orchestra contains four movements of which the first three were also published with organ
accompaniment, and the fourth, written later than the others, is
a fugue.

Of the works with organ accompaniment the three Motets, Op.
39, contain some fresh and pleasant music, though there is nothing
of outstanding interest; the most extended movement is the spirited
fugal finale of the third. *Hear my Prayer* and the *Te Deum* in A
were both written in England; despite the enormous popularity of
the former, the more dignified and less mellifluous *Te Deum* is on
the whole the better work. The *Responsorium et Hymnus*, Op. 121,
for men's voices, cellos and basses, is a quite successful essay in an
archaic manner. On the other hand the three Psalms for unaccompanied double choir, Op. 78, though severely restrained in
their idiom, have no suggestion of archaism. The second is a
setting of Psalm XLIII; for the final verses, beginning 'My soul,
why art thou so disquieted,' Mendelssohn quotes from the music
that he had used for the equivalent verses in his earlier setting of
Psalm XLII; its treatment here is less pretentious and more effective.
All three have considerable beauty and dignity, especially, perhaps,
the setting of Psalm II, which has an ingenious four-part canon for
its Gloria. Similar qualities are to be found in the third of the
three Motets, Op. 23, *Mitten wir im Leben sind*, an austere and
impressive piece of writing, and, on a smaller scale, in the six
short Motets, Op. 79. The remaining works for unaccompanied
chorus, which include settings of the *Nunc Dimittis*, *Jubilate*, and
Magnificat, Op. 69, are on the whole less distinctive, though the
general level is higher than that of the works with organ accompaniment. The first Motet from Op. 23, *Aus tiefer Not*, is in
five sections, of which four are unaccompanied and built upon
the familiar chorale. Here Mendelssohn imitates the idiom of

Bach with considerable success, especially in the second, which is a fugue. The third section, which is accompanied and has no connection with the chorale, is in Mendelssohn's more usual style and therefore not very suitable to its surroundings. In the second Motet, *Ave Maria*, which has an accompaniment either for organ or for clarinets, bassoons, cellos and basses, there is again a rather marked contrast between the pastoral simplicity of the opening and the contrapuntal texture of the central section, but the slightly elaborated return of the opening material prevents any possible sense of incongruity. The two *Festgesänge* for male voices and brass band are pompous *pièces de circonstance* of no great value. The second, composed for the Gutenberg Festival at Leipzig in 1840, contains the tune subsequently adapted to the hymn *Hark! the herald-angels sing*; this is undoubtedly better with Mendelssohn's original barring, but it is in any case more suitable as an invocation to 'Gutenberg, der deutsche Mann' than as a celebration of the birth of Christ.

CHAPTER XVI

MUSIC FOR THE STAGE

MENDELSSOHN'S interest in the stage was considerably livelier than might have been expected from the comparatively small amount of music that he wrote for it. His rather priggish comments on Auber's *Fra Diavolo* show that he had decided views on what was suitable for stage presentation, and he was continually on the watch for a libretto; if he had made the right choice he might have written an admirable opera, but much would have depended on the choice. *The Wedding of Camacho*, which was finished late in 1825, is lively, pleasant and thoroughly sure of itself, but far less individual than such contemporary instrumental works as the very spirited and original *Capriccio* in F sharp minor for piano. Here and there are turns of phrase that look ahead to later works, and in Quiteria's song in F minor we find the familiar combination of 6–8 time and the direction *agitato e presto*; but on the whole the music is steeped in Mozart and Weber. The use of the pompous phrase that heralds the entries of Don Quixote was claimed by Grove as the earliest employment of a Wagnerian *Leitmotiv*, but this view cannot be maintained in view of the very imaginative and resourceful treatment of themes in Weber's *Euryanthe*. The libretto, adapted by Klingemann from an amusing episode from *Don Quixote*, is rather heavy-footed, and the music, despite several attempts to capture a Spanish atmosphere, is too suggestive of a polite and well-behaved tea-party to be an ideal setting for the farcical and fantastic imaginings of Cervantes. It was first produced, after various difficulties and with qualified success, at Berlin in 1827;

145

the next performance, in 1885, took place, rather surprisingly, at Boston, U.S.A.

The operetta *Die Heimkehr aus der Fremde*, more commonly known as *Son and Stranger*, is a wholly delightful little work that deserves to be better known. The music still shows traces of Weber's influence, and the duet between Lisbeth and Ursula, the one gay and the other wistful, recalls Agathe and Ännchen in *Der Freischütz*. But there is far more individuality than in *Camacho*; this can be seen at once if their two overtures are compared. The earlier movement is brilliant and lively, but little more; in the other there are touches of poetry that are all the more effective for their lightness of hand. Lisbeth's solo 'So mancher zog in 's Weite' has an appealing simplicity, its unaccompanied end being particularly effective; the pedlar Kauz's song 'Ich bin ein vielgereister Mann' rivals Rossini in its resilient vivacity, and the slow mock-heroic passage near the end has an extravagance unusual for Mendelssohn. Hermann's first solo presents two contrasting moods with equal success, its quiet end being a particularly happy touch. The final section of the trio 'O wie verschweig' ich' is in Mendelssohn's liveliest scherzo manner, and equally characteristic is the very delicate orchestral writing in 'Es steigt das Geisterreich herauf.' After a picturesque orchestral interlude describing the sunrise, Lisbeth enters to the accompaniment of some phrases from the overture; her song 'Die Blumenglocken mit hellem Schein' shows that Klingemann could compose music in a quite convincingly Mendelssohnian style. The chorus that follows this has great delicacy and charm; the finale is pleasant but less distinguished. The libretto, a simple story of mistaken identity, provides chances for character drawing of which full advantage is taken, and the scene in which Hermann's singing is constantly interrupted by the pedlar seems almost to suggest the second act of *Die Meistersinger*. The work might still be worth reviving, though preferably in a translation other than that of H. F. Chorley, which contains such infelicities as 'One must

146

the flute and viols play' and 'When the moon begins to [pause] gleam.'

The remainder of Mendelssohn's works for the stage were written during the last seven years of his life. In the music composed for German translations of Sophocles' *Antigone* and *Oedipus at Colonus* there are good things, but they are surrounded by much that is pompous and perfunctory. *Antigone* is on the whole the better of the two; its introduction is in a dignified, almost tragic manner, but this soon gives place to the familiar and not very impressive *agitato* mood. Of the choruses the best are undoubtedly the fifth, which has a broadly flowing melody of greater rhythmic freedom than usual, and the third, the final section of which looks ahead, in its sombre energy, to the F minor Quartet. The second is in a gently lilting rhythm which is suitable enough for the sentiments expressed in the opening strophe, but quite inadequate for the later stages. In *Oedipus at Colonus* the level of musical invention is lower; in the setting of the third chorus, one of Sophocles' loveliest lyrics, the melody is disappointingly pedestrian, though it is effectively treated towards the end, and in the sixth Mendelssohn's favourite 6–8 rhythm is far from suitable to the resigned pessimism of the words. In the first, second and fourth choruses the frequent alternations of singing and speech are not very happy, but the seventh contains some music of real dramatic power, and the eighth has an impressive solemnity. But, with all their merits, these works both suggest that if Mendelssohn had written a successful opera it would not have been a tragedy, and this impression is confirmed by the music for Racine's *Athalie*, which, though solid and serious in aim, very seldom leaves the ground. The overture, a less imaginative relation of the first movement of the 'Reformation' Symphony, is followed by a chorus of which the very pompous main melody:

Allegro maestoso vivace

Tout l'u - ni-vers est plein de   sa mag - ni - fi - cen - ce

recurs with distressing frequency. The next movement has more variety; there is a pleasant lyrical flow in the setting of 'O, bien heureux mille fois,' and in the music that follows, culminating in a broad chorale-like melody, the tension is well sustained. But the rest of the work is for the most part very undistinguished, and the attempts to be dramatic, such as the accompaniment of Joad's declamation by a chorale melody played by a trumpet against a shimmering orchestral background, are not particularly happy. The once famous War March of the Priests does not now sound either warlike or priestly, and the chorus that follows it, with the frequent repetitions of 'Partez, partez, enfants d'Aaron, partez' against a curiously bolero-like accompaniment, comes perilously near to *The Pirates of Penzance*. The references to the opening theme of the overture are quite effective, but eventually the work ends, all too appropriately, with the pompous melody of the first chorus.

To turn from this to the incidental music to *A Midsummer Night's Dream* is to feel not only relief, but also astonishment that these two works should have been written by the same man at approximately the same period of his life. Of all Mendelssohn's later works, the *Midsummer Night's Dream* music provides the most convincing answer to those who regard his career as a gradual decline from genius to mediocrity, and it is amazing that he should have recaptured so vividly the mood of the overture that had been composed so many years before. The first entr'acte, which is the most extended of all his scherzos, seems to suggest every aspect of fairyland; the first theme its delicacy, the second its humour and several passages its more formidable side. The same delicacy is to be found in the delightful little march that accompanies the entry of Oberon and Titania and the setting of 'Ye spotted snakes,' with its very happy alternations of minor and major. In the second entr'acte the agitation of Hermia and Helena and the humours of Bottom and his friends are portrayed vividly and at the same time with exquisite lightness of touch; the third is the beautiful and familiar Nocturne. Apart from these extended movements there are many pieces of background music that are full of delightful effects, such as the distortion of the opening chords of the overture at the moment when Titania awakes and falls in love with Bottom. The last act is concerned mainly with the human characters, but Mendelssohn is here on as happy terms with them as with the fairies. The Wedding March, hackneyed though it has become, retains far more vitality than the more pretentious War March of the Priests from *Athalie*. Its opening, in which Mendelssohn plunges at once into a modulation that he had reserved for a special moment in the earlier Song without Words in A flat in Book IV, was for many years considered bold; it is eventually explained at the wonderful moment when the procession disappears into the distance and the C major of the march merges into the E minor of the fairy music. The Funeral March for Pyramus and Thisbe is an admirable piece of restrained comedy and the Bergomask Dance makes a very effective use of a theme from the overture. The finale is built upon the fairy music of the overture, with counter-melodies for the voices, and ending, inevitably, with the ethereal opening chords.

Of Mendelssohn's unfinished opera *Loreley* only three movements survive. Two of them, the 'Ave Maria' and the drinking-song, have an attractive simplicity, the former being entirely free from the sentimentality that might have been feared. The finale of the first act opens with great fire and excitement, but with the entry of Leonora, the heroine, the music seems somehow to lose its character, and the effect of the last section is somewhat spoilt by the rather pedestrian rhythm of its main theme. With the stage works may be included the ambitious but not very arresting concert aria *Infelice* and a slight but charming vocal duet intended for *Ruy Blas*.

CHAPTER XVII

GENERAL CHARACTERISTICS

EARLY in the nineteenth century the distinction between 'classical' and 'modern' was less strongly marked than it is at the present day, and it was easier for the average music-lover to enjoy the works of living and recently dead composers without relying so much for his daily bread on the masterpieces of the past. The year 1809 marks not only the birth of Mendelssohn but also the death of Haydn, whose music, however, like that of Mozart, was already widely known and loved. The existing works of Beethoven, for all their provocative qualities, were not as far removed from the everyday language of music as is much of the more provocative work of the twentieth century. It is not surprising that these composers should all, in different ways, have influenced Mendelssohn in his most impressionable years: of the younger men, Weber obviously made the strongest appeal, and his influence can be seen in many of the earlier works. He was keenly interested in the development of Beethoven's style and must have taken steps to become acquainted with his works as they came out; the most striking result of this is his Quartet in A minor, Op. 13, which is so strongly influenced by Beethoven's Op. 132, one of the most recent and progressive of his works. At that time, at any rate, he was far from being a reactionary in his tastes; in the other direction, it can be seen in a number of works that his knowledge of the music of J. S. Bach and D. Scarlatti was deeper than might well have been expected at that time, and that he possessed the power, by no means common in the nineteenth century, of writing in a contrapuntal style without an air of self-conscious archaism.

Elsewhere in this book individual instances have been produced of the influence of Beethoven on Mendelssohn, and it may be said in general that of his predecessors Beethoven was probably the one whom he was most eager to emulate, and with whom he had least in common temperamentally. This is most obvious on the all-too-frequent occasions on which Mendelssohn tries unsuccessfully to capture the serene and solemn mood of Beethoven's slow movements; in the vigorous and full-blooded rhetoric of the string Quartets in A minor and F minor, the first movement of the Trio in C minor and other works, he comes nearer to the spirit of Beethoven, though without his staying power. Beethoven, even at his most vehement, always seems to be holding something in reserve; Mendelssohn's passion is sincere and eloquent, but is not guided by the same firmly controlling hand. Nor had he Beethoven's skill in the invention and development of short, incisive rhythmic figures; the *Hebrides* overture is, of course, a supremely successful exception, and the first movement of the Quartet in E flat from Op. 44, though less imaginative, has something of the same power; but more often, as in the first movements of the piano Sonata in B flat and the *Hymn of Praise*, he is least inspired when most obviously trying to follow Beethoven's methods. He certainly never achieved the peculiarly dynamic collaboration between heart and mind that enabled Beethoven to explore so astonishingly wide an emotional range without loss of balance.

With Mozart he had more in common; both developed early and had an exceptionally fluent technique. Mendelssohn's development was far less steady; his early works contain things far more imaginative and individual than anything that Mozart wrote at the same age, but in later years, though they do not show the total decline that is sometimes imagined, his inspiration was undoubtedly more fitful. He could approach Mozart's polish and beauty, but he could not combine it in Mozart's unique way with a disturbingly intense personal emotion. Neither composer was a pioneer by temperament. Both thought naturally in terms of smoothly flowing melody, symmetrically rounded in design, but Mozart's melodic language was the current idiom of his own day, often raised to a transcendently high level, Mendelssohn's, compared with that of his contemporaries, was already slightly old-fashioned. The tunes of Schubert, his senior by twelve years, have far greater variety of rhythmic structure; those of Chopin, only a year his junior, though usually regular in outline, have greater subtlety of detail, and those of Schumann, though sometimes square to a fault, have a curious, wayward character of their own. Beside these the tunes of Mendelssohn, for all their attractiveness, seem far more limited in scope, less varied in melodic curve and rhythmic impetus. Even Haweis, one of his most devoted admirers, admitted, in *Music and Morals*, that

> The quality, at once delicate, tender and sublime, of Mendelssohn's creations is not questioned; but the endless though bewitching repetitions, or inversions of the same phrase, and an identity of form which amounts to more than a mannerism, compel us to admit that the range of his musical ideas was limited.

It would be interesting to know whether Mendelssohn was well acquainted with *Così fan tutte*; if so, he must have made a special response to the lovely opening phrase:

of the duet with chorus in the second act; it is curious to see how many echoes of it are to be found in his works:

Of these themes some have greater distinction than others, but they all show how he tended unconsciously to repeat the same melodic patterns. Rhythmically he is also inclined to overwork certain familiar gambits. One of the most characteristic is to be found in the melody from the introduction of the *Rondo capriccioso* quoted in the chapter on the piano music; two phrases, both beginning on the third beat of a common-time bar, the first with a 'feminine,' the second with a 'masculine' end. This occurs very frequently, the slow movement of the D minor Trio and the Song without Words, Op. 30, No. 3, illustrating it with particular clarity; it may have had some connection in Mendelssohn's mind with the metre of the heroic couplet. The drooping two-note figure, e.g.: , with which his phrases so often end, is liable to impair their vitality, especially when the music is in a quick tempo. Mention has

already been made of the similarity and difference between the
first movements of the 'Italian' Symphony and the cello Sonata
in D; this can be clearly illustrated by a comparison of the main
themes:

The theme from the cello Sonata, for all its vivacity, has not
quite the exhilarating resilience of that of the 'Italian' Symphony,
and this is largely due to the frequent feminine endings of the
phrases. Mendelssohn's fondness for tunes that begin half-way
through a bar, after the manner of a gavotte, is so pronounced as
to be a mannerism, but it probably arose from a desire to prevent
the rhythms from becoming too square, and if his intentions are
carefully observed, with a sensitive distinction between strong and
less strong beats, there is certainly less danger of the rhythms
becoming pedestrian.

It is easy now to be aware of the limitations of Mendelssohn's
thematic invention, especially when it is put beside that of some
of his contemporaries, but that is only one side of the question.
During the nineteenth century composers were increasingly concerned with their own individuality, but in the eighteenth they
were less self-conscious and less frightened of repeating themselves
or of using the same language as their less ambitious contemporaries. In Mendelssohn there was a strong streak of romanticism, but there was also much that was temperamentally more
akin to the eighteenth century, and he certainly had neither the

strength nor the weakness of the pioneer. If his work is judged on its own merits, without irrelevant comparisons, though it may be claimed that he did not always put his ideas to the best pur, pose, and that their quality is decidedly variable, it is impossible to deny the shapeliness and charm of his melody at its best. It flows most easily in a gently lyrical mood, but sometimes, as in the Prelude in E minor and the main part of the finale of the 'Scottish' Symphony, it can appear with equal success in more fiery and impetuous moods. In the finest specimens the beauty of the melodic line softens the general regularity of structure. Although he had not the literary sensitiveness of Schubert or Schumann, he could sometimes be stimulated by the problems of setting metrical verse into a greater rhythmic flexibility than usual, as in *Das erste Veilchen, Die Liebende schreibt* and the solemn and moving final stanza of *Nachtlied*. The ease and suavity of his melody is a thing that has been valued very differently at different times. It made a particularly strong appeal in England during his lifetime and for many years afterwards, especially among those who still found the more adventurous romantics difficult to approach; it could be accepted as being at the same time sympathetic and contemporary in circles where Mozart was considered pretty and old, fashioned and was, of course, followed by many inferior imitations. A melodic gift that flows easily and persuasively on accepted lines can be overrated by the semi, musical, but it is often in danger of being underrated by the more hard, bitten professional. When it leaves a sense of inadequacy in Mendelssohn's music it does so because it is not strong enough or varied enough to be always satisfactory for the purposes for which he uses it.

His harmonic idiom, though easily recognized, is less easy to describe than might be expected. The chromaticism that is so characteristic of the latest works of Mozart was developing in various ways in the first half of the nineteenth century. Mozart's own use of it was highly fastidious, and it is significant that the most highly coloured instances of it tend to come in quick rather than slow movements. Spohr handled it with far less restraint, and its appearances in his music are too frequent to be very effective. In some of Mendelssohn's early slow movements, such as those of the Symphony in C minor and the piano Quartet in F minor, the chromaticism is reminiscent of Mozart; in the *andante* of the B minor Quartet it is more akin to Spohr in its luxuriance. But on the whole chromatic colour does not play an outstandingly important part in Mendelssohn's music; he never used it with anything like as much freedom or imagination as Chopin.

The diminished seventh inevitably plays an important part; sometimes it brings a feeling of Brahmsian mystery, as in the slow section of the *Fantasia* or *Caprice* in A minor from Op. 16, or of Beethovenish defiance, as at the climax before the pause in the Fugue in F minor from Op. 35 or the coda of the *Variations sérieuses*. Weakly sentimental uses of it, such as:

are rather less common than is often supposed, and it is frequently used with considerable power with a dissonant note below, as in the scherzo of the F minor string Quartet. Inversions of the dominant seventh, so beloved by composers of Victorian hymn tunes, occur frequently. Mendelssohn is particularly fond of the first inversion; when this occurs just before a cadence, as at the end of 'O rest in the Lord,' the result is often rather cloying. On the other hand its frequent appearance in the Song without Words in G from Op. 53 gives the piece an attractively individual character, and it often appears, with admirable effect, as an unexpected touch in a slightly altered repetition of a phrase, as in:

He is also fond of the minor chord of the subdominant, though it plays a less important part in his music than in that of Brahms. His use of modulation is less enterprising than that of his contemporaries, to say nothing of Schubert, but there are moments, such as the wonderful opening of the development of the *Hebrides* overture, that have a touch of Schubertian fantasy and would not seem out of place in a mature work of Wagner or Bruckner.

His harmony often depends for its success on the texture in which it is presented. He was obviously attracted by the broad and dignified effects that Beethoven frequently produced with simple block harmony, but his own attempts to emulate these are usually unsuccessful and tend either to amble amiably, like the opening of the slow movement of the C minor Trio, or to stagnate, as in the main theme of the *adagio* of the *Hymn of Praise*. On the other hand he is decidedly happy in the invention of accompanying figures that are mainly harmonic in character but not mere formulae; there are many instances of these in the Songs without Words, including several cases in which the accompaniment has more character than the tune. He was a fluent and able contrapuntist, and the presence of any contrapuntal element often enlivens the harmonic colour of his music: a pleasant instance is the Prelude in A flat from Op. 35, where the two melodic parts singing contrapuntally against a persistent accompaniment produce attractive harmonic clashes. Effects of this kind usually occur when the music is contrapuntal, but sometimes they appear in a more harmonic texture, resulting from persistent pedal-notes, usually in the top or inner parts. Two instances in very different moods from piano works are worth quoting:

Passages of this kind suggest the influence of Domenico Scarlatti, many of whose boldest harmonic effects derive similarly from persistent and unexpected pedal-points. Mendelssohn in his best works sometimes produced an impression of remarkable spaciousness by broadening the harmonic motion; there are fine examples in the development sections of the *Midsummer Night's Dream* and *Hebrides* overtures.

His handling of form is less adventurous than that of most of the romantics, particularly in his later works, but it can seldom be described as mechanically conservative. The recapitulation is the feature of the classical sonata form that has undergone most modification, and in several of Mendelssohn's earlier works, such as the *Hebrides* overture and the first movements of the Octet, the string Quintet in A and the piano Sonata in E, it is handled with remarkable freedom, and even in later works it is often less regular than might be expected. Mendelssohn often shortens the space between the first and second subjects and is fond of bringing back some of the omitted material in the coda. He often gives unity to the exposition by concluding it with a reminiscence of the first subject; this is done particularly imaginatively in the first movement of the 'Italian' Symphony. The return to the main theme is almost always contrived particularly well. Some-times, as in the first movements of the Octet and the 'Italian' Symphony, it is introduced by a long *crescendo*, in an atmosphere of Beethoven-like suspense, but more often it happens quietly, with some new harmonic or contrapuntal feature. In the first movements of the Trio in D minor and the 'Scottish' Symphony there is a new counter-melody, but more often the change is harmonic, the chord of the tonic in root position being usually avoided. Perhaps the most striking instance is in the F minor string Quartet, where it happens at the height of a climax, with different harmony below and a counter-melody above. Passages of this kind are unusual for the time; as a rule the return to the main theme in the tonic key was regarded as a dramatic event, but Mendelssohn aims at making the hearer realize that he has reached home without knowing clearly how it happened. Some-times it involves a slowing down of the harmonic movement, as in the scherzo of the Octet and the delightful fourth piece from Op. 7; sometimes, as in the fourth Song without Words from Op. 85, it is done with an ingeniously contrived air of casual-ness that seems almost to point to the methods of Debussy. It is, however, characteristic of Mendelssohn that the most individual feature of his treatment of musical form should be concerned with a particular detail rather than with general principles.

A general survey of his output leaves an odd mixture of im-pressions. He had many distinguished contemporaries,[1] and it was therefore almost inevitable that for several generations posterity should judge them all by similar standards. The result of this was that Mendelssohn was perpetually taken to task for his com-parative unadventurousness, and his merits were often either

[1] See the first ten years of the Calendar, Appendix A.

ignored or underrated. But his own contemporaries saw him from a very different angle. Berlioz, who could certainly not be described as a reactionary, wrote in the most enthusiastic terms of *Die erste Walpurgisnacht*, which he regarded as a masterpiece of romanticism. To the London critic H. F. Chorley, as is shown by a passage already quoted, Mendelssohn was definitely one of the 'moderns,' interesting and well worth study, but often difficult and complex, and far less easy of approach than Mozart. He is, of course, far from being the only composer who has been praised and blamed for entirely contradictory reasons at different times; the same has happened to Brahms, and during the last three decades fashions have changed so often that the modernisms of to-day may seem outmoded the day after to-morrow. But in the case of Mendelssohn it is due to some extent to the fact that, in spite of his great gifts, there were in him certain conflicts that were never completely resolved. His father's well-meant advice to be solid and serious at all costs, and the popularity of the oratorio in England, both led him along paths that were not entirely suited to his natural bent. His technique in composition never faltered, but emotionally he was liable to hover rather uneasily between the polished clarity of the eighteenth and the more luxuriant emotionalism of the nineteenth century. In the finest of the early works there is no trace of this, the music being at the same time very original in conception and presented with the greatest ease and smoothness. Before long he seems often to be worried by an urge towards a more passionate emotional expression that is constantly thwarted. It is interesting to compare for a minute the fiery and high-spirited *Capriccio* in F sharp minor, Op. 5, composed in 1825, with the *Capriccio* in B flat minor from Op. 33, which was written in 1833. The slow introduction of the later work has a sombre and massive dignity of which there is no trace in Op. 5 or indeed in any of the earlier works; but as soon as the quick section begins, something seems to have gone out of the music, which merely runs about with much agitation after nothing in particular. The unpleasant adjective 'smug' has been frequently applied to Mendelssohn's music, and it is difficult to avoid when contemplating certain works, but it is misleading, as it implies a streak of passive stolidity that was certainly not in his make-up. One of the most obvious features of his life was his restlessness, his perpetual expense of energy, sometimes on trivial purposes, and when his music is at its weakest, this is due less to self-satisfaction than to a desire to squeeze from his ideas more intensity than is inherent in them. Sometimes he reminds us of certain characters of Jane Austen such as Mr. Collins or Miss Bates, who, in the words of Mr. J. B. Priestley, 'contrive to be excited about nothing.'

At this point it is worth remembering for a moment that for many years Mozart was regarded with something of the same patronizing attitude that is now often taken towards Mendelssohn; this suggests that history might repeat itself and that Mendelssohn might eventually take as high a place as Mozart does at the moment. On the whole it is unlikely; the two had obvious points of resemblance, and in Mozart's work there is something of the same suggestion of conflict between the claims of formal elegance and emotional expression. So exquisite, however, is his sense of style that it remains a suggestion and no more, the various elements of his personality and background being perfectly integrated. Mendelssohn, beginning more brilliantly, never reached the same degree of maturity. But his later work, for all its inequality, has often been dismissed far too summarily and is at the moment most inadequately known. The music to *A Midsummer Night's Dream* shows that he could on occasion recapture with complete success the atmosphere of his early masterpieces. But this is not all; there was undoubtedly an undercurrent of surprisingly sombre emotion, considerably deeper than the rather ineffectively restless agitation with which we are so much more familiar. There is a tantalizingly brief glimpse of it at the beginning of the *Capriccio* in B flat minor; it appears with surprising ferocity in the *Volkslied* from the fourth book of Songs without Words, with cumulative dramatic power in several of the choruses from *Elijah*, with dignified resignation in the *Nachtlied* and, most fully of all, in that startlingly stormy and passionate swan-song, the string Quartet in F minor.

The high quality of his orchestration, clear, economical and sometimes surprisingly imaginative, has never been questioned; still less the brilliant originality of his scherzos. The streak of rather sanctimonious sentimentality that spoils a certain amount of his slow music is undoubtedly a blemish, but it has sometimes been exaggerated; it appears at its worst in some of the weaker solos from the choral works. But there are many lyrical movements, both vocal and instrumental, from which it is entirely absent and which, under a rather conventionally 'pretty' exterior, still preserve a singularly appealing and heart-easing quality. These are some of the different facets of a composer whom, after much indiscriminate praise and blame, we are at last beginning to see from a more balanced perspective, and for whose best work we shall always feel a deep and lasting affection.

ADDENDA

OF THE various works of Mendelssohn that have been published during the last fifteen years, the earliest is the Concerto in D minor for violin and string orchestra, which was discovered and edited by Yehudi Menuhin. It was composed in 1822, a year after the early Sonata in G minor for piano. The two works have points in common: in both of them the outer movements are influenced by Haydn and Mozart, and the slow movement is more individual than the rest; but the Concerto is the stronger and more interesting work. The first movement gives ample evidence of Mendelssohn's love for Mozart's piano Concerto in D minor, which he often played with great success. Structurally the most original feature is the recapitulation; there is no pause for a cadenza, and the two main themes reappear in reverse order, the second going through some impressive modulations. The Finale is more Haydnesque, especially in the resourcefulness with which its single vivacious theme is treated. The slow movement comes considerably nearer to Mendelssohn's mature style; compared with that of the piano Sonata in G minor it is firmer in structure and more distinctive thematically, covering a wide range of keys. The coda has an impressive breadth, and a sustained high note played by the soloist leads into the finale in a manner prophetic of the note played by the bassoon that connects the first and second movements of the later violin Concerto.

Of the twelve Symphonies for string orchestra composed by Mendelssohn between 1821 and 1823, two have been recently published; of these the earlier, in D major, dates from 1822 and was later rewritten for full orchestra. It has several Haydnesque features: the slow introduction in the tonic minor which precedes the first movement, the fluent and lively contrapuntal writing, and the monothematic character of the two outer movements. The first *allegro* contains a subsidiary idea strongly reminiscent of the overture to *The Magic Flute* and the first movement of Mozart's 'Prague' Symphony. The most interesting portions of the work are the slow movement, in which there are no violins, and the violas are divided into three parts, and the very lively Trio of the Minuet. In the version for full orchestra, however, this is replaced by another Trio, perhaps less striking musically but charmingly scored. In this version of the slow movement there are still no violins, but the woodwind and horns provide a sensitively graded harmonic background. The slightly later Symphony in C, written in 1823, is a more enterprising work. Here again the first movement is monothematic and preceded by a slow introduction in the minor. In the slow movement Mendelssohn is still exploring the possibilities of varied string colour. The first section is for violins only, in four parts; the central episode is a threepart *fugato* for the lower strings, who reenter gradually during the *da capo* of the first section. For the last seven bars everyone luxuriates happily in the chord of E major. The Trio of the Scherzo, entitled *La Suisse*, is built on a yodelling tune which produces an attractively vague tonality. But the finale is the most ambitious part of the work. Unlike the first movement it contains three contrasting ideas, one rhythmic, one fugal and one lyrical, and there is much less of the influence of Mozart and Haydn than in most of Mendelssohn's previous works. The movement is overlong and the rhetoric sometimes empty, but it has remarkable vigour, and shows an increase of individuality, as in this very characteristic cadence:

Addenda

The chamber works written at about the same time as the Symphonies for strings include the piano Quartets in C minor and F minor, which show how strongly Mendelssohn was influenced by the brilliant keyboard writing of Weber. This is still more apparent in the Concertos in E and A flat for two pianos and orchestra, written in 1823 and 1824 respectively. They do not approach in imaginativeness such a work as the *Rondo Capriccioso* for piano, or the slightly later *Capriccio* in F sharp minor, but they contain some agreeable and characteristic music. The presence of two soloists and the necessity of providing brilliant solo passages for both of them leads inevitably to great length, and in the first movement of the E major Concerto the very leisurely *tutti* and exposition set a standard of spaciousness which Mendelssohn is not able to maintain in the later stages of the movement, and the general result is rather lopsided. The first movement of the A flat Concerto is longer still, but better balanced; its opening is not unlike that of Field's piano Concerto in the same key. The slow movements are both in a quietly flowing 6–8 time, combining a gentle lyricism prophetic of some of the Songs without Words with much decorative writing for the two soloists. The Finale of the E major Concerto is a lively and entertaining patchwork with constant contrast between brilliant and more lyrical ideas. That of the A flat Concerto has more character; the tonal scheme of the opening theme almost suggests a hilarious parody of the opening of Beethoven's *Waldstein* Sonata, and there is some very effective fugal writing. Of the two Concertos the second is certainly the more satisfactory work, and is well worth an occasional revival.

The clarinet Sonata in E flat, which dates from about 1825, is an interesting but unequal work. The exposition of the first movement is overladen with empty passage work, but the development section has remarkable power and concentration. Here the first bar of the seemingly amiable main theme is made the basis of a fiercely insistent dialogue which rises to a climax followed by an impressive *diminuendo*. But the most striking feature of the work is the haunting theme of the slow movement, played first by the clarinet unaccompanied.

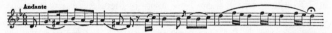

The reiterated rhythm in bars four and five plays an important role, not only in the clarinet melody but also in the piano part, which contains some curious rhapsodical passages. The finale is more conventional in its material but, like the first movement, it has an exciting and eventful development, largely contrapuntal in texture, which leads, as so often in Mendelssohn, to a beautifully contrived return. Looking back at the Sonata as a whole, its inequalities are nothing like as pronounced as those of the slightly earlier Sextet for piano and strings, though it does not reach the level of the piano Quartet in B minor. But, despite reminiscences of Mozart and Weber, the idiom is generally individual and the manner pleasantly fresh and lyrical.

The violin Sonata in F is a much later work, written in 1838. Its nearest neighbour among the chamber works is the cello Sonata in B flat, and the two works differ exactly as might be expected from the character of their respective instruments, the one being as obviously inspired by the brilliance and agility of the violin as is the other by the mellow warmth of the cello. The opening theme of the violin Sonata starts half way through the bar in a manner very characteristic of Mendelssohn; it has great vigour and contrasts well with the flowing and rather more conventional melody of the second group. The movement is spacious both in style and in dimensions; the development is full of incident, and the opening of the recapitulation, in which the first theme is played by the piano to a background of violin arpeggios, is strongly prophetic of the equivalent passage in the violin Concerto in E minor. The coda opens impressively with a reminiscence of a passage from the development, and the brilliant piano writing is admirably organized. The *adagio* is richly coloured, with a luxuriance not unlike that of Weber, though perhaps more firmly controlled. The entry of the violin—a bar sooner than one would expect—is, for Mendelssohn, an unusual feature which recurs in the finale. In many ways this is one of the most remarkable of his slow movements; it contains several passages of a strikingly passionate nature, and is broadly and skilfully designed. The finale is in a lighter vein than the other two, but is brilliantly animated; the constant interweaving of the violin and piano parts gives it a distinction less in evidence in some of Mendelssohn's later finales in a similar mood, such as those of the cello Sonata in D and the string Quintet in B flat. The Sonata as a whole is one of the best instrumental works of its period, and it is surprising that its composer apparently did not consider it worthy of publication.

Since the above was written, several more early works by Mendelssohn have been published. The largest is the one-act operetta *Die Beiden Pedagogen*, composed in 1821, the libretto having been adapted by J. L. Kaspar from a comedy by Scribe called *Les Deux Precepteurs*. For the work of a boy of twelve, this is an astonishingly able production; the style is not particularly individual, but the technique is brilliantly accomplished, sometimes with an almost Rossinian sparkle and humour. The Overture opens with a reminiscence, probably accidental, of the 'Réjouissance' from Handel's 'Music for the Royal Fireworks.' The bass solo for Kinderschreck, the schoolmaster, 'Probatum est,' has an amusingly pedagogic ring, and later on there is an ensemble in which he and Luftig, the valet disguised as a schoolmaster, argue heatedly over the respective merits of the educational systems of Pestalozzi and Basedow. The melodic invention, as Devrient remarks, is not very striking, but the gusto and vivacity of the music are attractive and the operetta might still be effective in a stage production.

The twelve Symphonies for strings are now all in print, and throw fascinating light on the early stages of Mendelssohn's development. The first five, which can be examined as a group, contain three movements, of which the first and last are all in a binary form that comes far nearer to the Baroque suite than to the classical sonata. The texture is solidly contrapuntal, in a style which would have sounded academic and old-fashioned at the time. But there is a remarkable skill and fluency, with a few original touches, such as the amusing 'coup de théâtre' with which the Finale of the first Symphony opens. The slow movements are more varied and more individual. That of the second Symphony is full of contrapuntal devices, but in a gently elegiac mood some way removed from the rather impersonal energy of the outer movements. The texture is beautifully woven, a rather perfunctory end being the only weakness. The other slow movements come nearer to Mendelssohn's more familiar lyrical vein; they are all in 3–8 time and look ahead to such things as the Adagio of the first organ Sonata. The most striking of them is that of the fourth Symphony, in which the melody is supported by a luxuriant background of arpeggios; there is also a very characteristic return of the main theme. Here, for the first time in these Symphonies, Mendelssohn explores the possibilities of rich colour; it is done with more variety in several of the later ones.

In the sixth Symphony, in E flat, the style begins to change. The first movement is less monothematic than the earlier ones; it is definitely in Sonata form, and more varied in its texture. The second movement is a Minuet, robust and laconic, with two trios. In the first of these the violas play a prominent part and in the second, phrases of a chorale-like melody alternate with vigorous contrapuntal passages which increase in length and at one moment look back to the Minuet. When the chorale is finished the contrapuntal passages become increasingly exuberant and lead, not to the expected 'da capo,' but to the Finale. Here Mendelssohn approaches the problem that had been so beautifully solved by Mozart in his String Quartet in G, K.382: that of combining Sonata form with a certain amount of fugal writing. This Finale opens in a lively and thoroughly post-Baroque manner, with a theme consisting mainly of rushing scale-passages; these appear from time to time in the rather self-consciously fugal second group. If the movement as a whole is not a complete success, its high spirits are engaging and very characteristic. But the seventh Symphony, in D minor, is a stronger and more ambitious work, and here for the first time there are four movements. There is also an increased resourcefulness in the handling of the medium. The first movement has some striking passages in which slowly moving sustained phrases are played against a background of staccato notes. The main theme of the Andante, a very attractive movement, is first played by the violins in two-part harmony, the lower instruments entering surreptitiously as the music proceeds; there is also a wider range of modulation. The Trio of the Minuet has a very unusual theme consisting of three rising thirds; it is frequently inverted, and, after the very emphatic end of the Trio, there is no indication of 'da capo.' In the Finale Mendelssohn returns to the problem that he has already approached in the previous Symphony, the combination of Sonata form with fugal writing. An introductory passage leads to a lively, galloping main theme; the second group begins fugally, but, as in so many of Mendelssohn's first movements, the exposition ends with a reference to the first theme. The two ideas are combined contra-puntally in both the development and the recapitulation. This Finale is certainly more firmly integrated than that of the sixth Symphony, and it ends with a most exhilarating climax.

The eighth and ninth Symphonies have already been described; the inclusion of a Swiss yodelling song in the latter was obviously a result of the family visit to Switzerland in 1822. The tenth, in B minor, consists of a single spaciously planned movement in Sonata form, preceded by a slow introduction that, with its expressive chromaticism, is reminiscent of the later works. Though very effective, the Symphony as a whole is less striking than the eleventh, which is the most remarkable of them all. It is an enormous

work in five movements. Though it is in F minor, the first move‑
ment is preceded by a slow introduction in F major, an unusual
feature which may have been suggested to Mendelssohn by Beet‑
hoven's 'Kreutzer' Sonata; it recurs in some of his piano works,
such as the Rondo Capriccioso. This introduction is remarkably
atmospheric and imaginative; it makes a very effective return
towards the end of the vigorous monothematic Allegro. The
Scherzo is an amusing attempt to suggest an exotic local colour;
like the Trio of the Scherzo of the ninth Symphony, it is based on
a Swiss tune, which in this case has slightly modal implications;
on its return the strings are joined by tympani, triangle and cymbals.
The Adagio, though owing something to early Beethoven, has
decidedly individual touches; the following

might well have caused the raising of more conservative eyebrows.
The fourth movement, though entitled 'Minuet,' is, like that of
the slightly later Sextet, in 6–8 time; its Trio has a theme of
very Mendelssohnian shape, similar to those quoted in Chapter
seventeen. The Finale is an elaborate movement in Sonata form,
with much vigorous fugal writing, and some impressive moments
of quiet suspense that look ahead to the Octet.

The twelfth Symphony, in G minor, though far from uninter‑
esting, is rather more impersonal than the eleventh. The form
of the first movement looks back to that of the eighteenth‑century
French Overture, a slow introduction leading to a Fugue. This
is built on a chromatic subject which has been anticipated towards
the end of the introduction; it is treated very resourcefully, with
inversion, augmentation and diminution, and the movement ends
with a powerful climax. The Finale, like that of the eleventh

Symphony, is in Sonata form, with much fugal writing; as in so many later works, there is a particularly impressive passage just before the recapitulation. The slow movement is gentle and intimate; its mood and texture are rather like those of the slow movement of Mozart's String Quartet in E flat, K.428. In addition to these twelve Symphonies there is a separate movement for string orchestra in C minor. This, like the first movement of the twelfth Symphony, is a Fugue preceded by a slow introduction, but is on a far larger scale. Here, without having recourse to the ingenious devices of the earlier Fugue, Mendelssohn builds up a large structure of great breadth and power, with unflagging energy and variety of texture. The publication of these works has been of particular interest in showing that, some time before he had reached the level of his finest early works, Mendelssohn was already an astonishingly precocious and accomplished crafts-man.

APPENDICES

APPENDIX A

CALENDAR

(Figures in brackets denote the age reached by the person mentioned during the year in question.)

Year	Age	Life	Contemporary Musicians
1809		Jakob Ludwig Felix Mendelssohn (Mendelssohn-Bartholdy) born, Feb. 3, at Hamburg, son of Abraham Mendelssohn (33), banker.	Haydn (77) dies, May 31. Adam aged 6; Attwood 44; Auber 27; Balfe 1; Beethoven 39; Bellini, 8; Benedict 5; Berlioz 6; Bishop 23; Boieldieu 34; Catel 36; Cherubini 49; Clementi 57; Donizetti 12; Dussek 48; Field 27; Glinka 6; Gossec 75 Grétry 68; Halévy 10; Hérold 18; Hummel 31; Lesueur 49; Loewe 13; Lortzing 6; Marschner 14; Méhul 46; Mercadante 14; Meyerbeer 18; Onslow 25; Paer 38; Paisiello 68; Rossini 17; Schubert 12; Spohr 25; Spontini 35; Vogler 60; Weber 23; Wesley (S.) 43; Zelter 51.
1810	1		Chopin born, Feb. 22; Nicolai born, June 9; Schumann born, June 8;

Year	Age	Life	Contemporary Musicians
			Wesley (S. S.) born, Aug. 14.
1811	2		Hiller born, Oct. 24; Liszt born, Oct. 22; Thomas (Ambroise) born, Aug. 5.
1812	3	Removal of the family to Berlin.	Dussek (51) dies, March 20; Flotow born, April 27; Wallace (Vincent) born, March 11.
1813	4		Dargomizhsky born, Feb. 2/14; Grétry (72) dies, Sept. 24; Macfarren born, March 2; Smart (Henry) born, Oct. 26; Verdi born, Oct. 10; Wagner born, May 22.
1814	5		Vogler (65) dies, May 6.
1815	6	Begins to learn the piano from his mother.	Franz born, June 28; Heller born, May 15.
1816	7	Visit to Paris. Lessons from Marie Bigot (30).	Bennett (Sterndale) born, April 13; Paisiello (75) dies, June 5.
1817	8	Begins to learn composition from Zelter (59).	Gade born, Feb. 22; Méhul (54) dies, Oct. 18.
1818	9	First public appearance at a chamber concert, Oct. 28.	Gounod born, June 17.
1819	10	Enters the Singakademie, April 11.	Offenbach born, June 21.
1820	11	Composes much. First dated work a cantata, Jan. 13.	Serov born, Jan. 11 23; Vieuxtemps born, Feb. 20.
1821	12	Numerous compositions. Piano Quartet, C minor (Op. 1). Meeting with Weber (35) and Benedict	

Year	Age	Life	Contemporary Musicians
		(17). Zelter (63) takes him to Weimar to see Goethe (72).	
1822	13	Visit to Switzerland. Meeting with Spohr (38) at Cassel and Hiller (11) at Frankfort.	Franck born, Dec. 19; Raff born, May 27.
1823	14	Has a private orchestra and continues to compose much. Piano Quartet, F minor (Op. 2).	Lalo born, Jan. 27.
1824	15	Visit of Moscheles (30), who gives M. lessons. Symphony No. 1, C minor.	Bruckner born, Sept. 4; Cornelius born, Dec. 24; Reinecke born, June 23; Smetana born, March 2.
1825	16	Visit to Paris, spring. Meeting with Cherubini (65), who greatly encourages him, also with Halévy (26), Herz (19), Kalkbrenner (39), Meyerbeer (34), Onslow (41), Paer (54), Rossini (33) and others. Piano Quartet (Op. 3) dedicated to Goethe (76). Opera, *Die Hochzeit des Camacho*, performance of which Spontini (51) seeks to prevent. Octet for strings (Op. 20).	Strauss (Johann ii) born, Oct. 25.
1826	17	Overture to *A Midsummer Night's Dream*.	Weber (40) dies, June 4/5.
1827	18	*Die Hochzeit des Camacho* produced at a minor Berlin theatre. String Quartet, A minor (Op. 13); Fugue, E	Beethoven (57) dies, March 26.

Year	Age	Life	Contemporary Musicians
		minor for piano (Op. 35, No. 1); piano Sonata, B flat major (Op. 106).	
1828	19	Overture, *Calm Sea and Prosperous Voyage*	Schubert (31) dies, Nov. 19.
1829	20	Conducts Bach's St. Matthew Passion at the Singakademie, March 11. Meeting with Paganini (45). First visit to England, April. Conducts for the first time in London, a concert of the Philharmonic Society, May 25. Friendship with Attwood (64). String Quartet, E flat major (Op. 12). Return to Berlin, Nov. Operetta, *Die Heimkehr aus der Fremde.*	Gossec (95) dies, Feb. 16.
1830	21	Symphony, D major ('Reformation'); Fantasy for piano, F sharp minor (Op. 28). Visit to Italy, autumn. Overture, *Hebrides (Fingal's Cave)* in its first form, Dec.	Catel (57) dies, Nov. 29; Goldmark born, May 18; Rubinstein born, Nov. 16/28.
1831	22	Meets Berlioz (28) in Rome, March. 'Scottish' and 'Italian' Symphonies begun in Italy. Returns to Germany via Switzerland, autumn. Piano Concerto, G minor (Op. 25). M. plays it for the first time, in Munich, Oct. 17. Visit to Paris, where he meets Liszt (20), Dec.	

Year	Age	Life	Contemporary Musicians
1832	23	Makes the acquaintance of Chopin (22) in Paris, Jan. Goes to England, April. Meeting with Field (50) in London. *Capriccio brillant* for piano and orchestra (Op. 22), first book of Songs without Words for piano and revised version of *Hebrides* (*Fingal's Cave*) overture written in London. Return to Berlin, July.	Clementi (80) dies, March 10; Zelter (74) dies, May 15.
1833	24	'Italian' Symphony finished, March 13. Third and fourth visits to London, April-May and June-Aug. Meeting with Hummel (55), Maria-Felicità Malibran (25) and Wilhelmine Schröder-Devrient (29). M. conducts the Lower Rhine Festival at Düsseldorf, May. He moves from Berlin to Düsseldorf, where he is appointed general musical director, autumn. Overture, *Die schöne Melusine*.	Brahms born, May 7; Hérold (42) dies, Jan. 19.
1834	25	*Rondo brillant* for piano and orchestra (Op. 29); *Infelice* for soprano and orchestra; *St. Paul* begun.	Boieldieu (59) dies, Oct. 8; Borodin born, Oct. 31/Nov. 12; Ponchielli born, Sept. 1.
1835	26	Leaves Düsseldorf for Leipzig, where he is appointed conductor of the	Bellini (34) dies, Sept. 24; Saint-Saëns born, Oct. 9.

Year	Age	Life	Contemporary Musicians
		Gewandhaus concerts, Aug. First meeting with Schumann (25), Oct. 3. Death of father, Abraham Mendelssohn (59), Nov. 19.	
1836	27	Meeting with Wagner (23), April. *St. Paul* finished, spring, and first performed at the Lower Rhine Festival at Düsseldorf, May 22. Visit to Frankfort and engagement there to Cécile Jeanrenaud (*c.* 17).	Balakirev born, Dec. 31 (O.S.).
1837	28	Friendship with Sterndale Bennett (21). Marriage to Cécile Jeanrenaud (*c.* 18), March 28. Psalm XLII, string Quartet, E minor (Op. 44, No. 2), piano Concerto, D minor, 3 Preludes for organ (Op. 37) composed, spring and summer. Visit to London, Aug. Oratorio on subject of Elijah planned. Conducts Birmingham Festival, including *St. Paul*, Sept. 19–21. Return to Leipzig. Preludes and Fugues for piano (Op. 35) published.	Field (55) dies, Jan. 11; Guilmant born, March 12; Jensen born, Jan. 12; Wesley (S.) (71) dies, Oct. 11.
1838	29	String Quartets (Op. 44, Nos. 1 and 3), cello Sonata, B flat major (Op. 45), Psalm XCV, violin	Attwood (73) dies, March 24; Bizet born, Oct. 25; Bruch born, Jan. 6.

Year	Age	Life	Contemporary Musicians
		Sonata, F major, *Serenade and Allegro gioioso* for piano and orchestra (Op. 43). Violin Concerto begun. Schumann (28) sends him Schubert's C major Symphony, discovered in Vienna, autumn.	
1839	30	Overture to *Ruy Blas*, March; Psalm CXIV, spring; piano Trio, D minor (Op. 49), July.	Mussorgsky born, March 9/21; Paer (68) dies, May 3; Rheinberger born, March 17.
1840	31	*Lobgesang (Hymn of Praise)* and *Festgesang* written for commemoration of the invention of printing, June 24–5. Visit to England and performance of the *Hymn of Praise* at the Birmingham Festival, Sept. 23.	Stainer born, June 6; Tchaikovsky born, April 25/May 7.
1841	32	Is appointed director of the music section of the Academy of Arts in Berlin, May. Sophocles' *Antigone* with music by M. performed at Potsdam, Oct. 28. *Variations sérieuses* for piano.	Chabrier born, Jan. 18; Dvořák born, Sept. 8; Pedrell born, Feb. 19.
1842	33	'Scottish' Symphony finished, Jan. 20; produced in Leipzig, March 3; conducted by M. at the Philharmonic Society in London, June 13. *Christmas Pieces* for piano (Op.	Boito born, Feb. 24; Cherubini (82) dies, March 15; Massenet born, May 12; Sullivan born, May 13.

Year	Age	Life	Contemporary Musicians
		72) written in London. Visit to Queen Victoria (23), June 20. Return to Germany, July. King of Prussia commissions music for Racine's *Athalie*, Shakespeare's *Midsummer Night's Dream* and Sophocles' *Oedipus at Colonus*, Nov. Return to Leipzig, where he founds the Conservatory, Nov. Meeting with Wagner (29).	
1843	34	Invites Berlioz (40) to Leipzig. Opening of the Conservatory there, April 3. Joachim (12) enters the institution. *A Midsummer Night's Dream*, with M.'s old overture and new incidental music, performed at Potsdam, Oct. Psalm II, Psalm XCVIII and cello Sonata, D major (Op. 58).	Grieg born, June 15; Sgambati born, May 28.
1844	35	Psalms XXII, XLIII and C, Jan.–March. English anthem, *Hear my Prayer*, Jan. 25. Visit to London to conduct five Philharmonic concerts, May–June. 6 organ Sonatas almost completed, July–Sept. Violin Concerto finished at Soden, Sept. 16. M. retires from Berlin and	Rimsky-Korsakov born, March 6/18.

Year	Age	Life	Contemporary Musicians
		settles at Frankfort in poor health, Dec.	
1845	36	Returns to the post of conductor of the Gewand-haus concerts at Leipzig, Sept. He teaches the piano and composition at the Conservatory there, of which he is virtually the director. String Quintet, B flat major (Op. 87); piano Trio, C minor (Op. 66).	Fauré born, May 13; Widor born, Feb. 22.
1846	37	*Lauda Sion* finished, Feb. 10. *Elijah* finished, late July. Departure for England, Aug., and first performance of *Elijah* at Birmingham Festival, Aug. 26. On his return, although in bad health, M. works exceedingly hard.	
1847	38	Composition of the opera, *Loreley*, to a libretto by Geibel (32) begun, also a new oratorio, *Christus*. M.'s health deteriorates more and more. Tenth visit to England, April - May. Death of his sister, Fanny Hensel (42), May 14. Visit to Switzerland, summer. At first too ill to do any work, he after-wards finishes the string	Mackenzie born, Aug. 22. Adam aged 44; Auber 65; Balakirev 11; Balfe 39; Benedict 43; Bennett 31; Berlioz 44; Bishop 61; Bizet 9; Boito 5; Borodin 3; Brahms 14; Bruch 9; Bruckner 23; Chabrier 6; Chopin 37; Cornelius 23; Dargomizhsky 34; Donizetti 50; Dvořák 6; Fauré 2; Flotow 35; Franck 25; Franz 32; Gade 30; Glinka

Year	Age	Life	Contemporary Musicians
		Quartet, F minor (Op. 80). Return to Leipzig exhausted, Sept. Mendelssohn dies in Leipzig, Nov. 4.	44; Goldmark 17; Gounod 29; Grieg 4; Guilmant 10; Halévy 48; Heller 32; Hiller 36; Jensen 10; Lalo 24; Liszt 36; Loewe 51; Lortzing 44; Macfarren 34; Marschner 52; Massenet 5; Mercadante 52; Meyerbeer 56; Mussorgsky 8; Nicolai 37; Offenbach 28; Onslow 63; Pedrell 6; Ponchielli 13; Raff 25; Reinecke 23; Rheinberger 8; Rimsky-Korsakov 3; Rossini 55; Rubinstein 17; Saint-Saëns 12; Schumann 37; Sgambati 4; Smetana 23; Spohr 63; Spontini 73; Stainer 7; Sullivan 5; Serov 27; Tchaikovsky 7; Thomas (A.) 36; Verdi 34; Wagner 34; Wallace 35; Wesley (S. S.) 37; Widor 2.

APPENDIX B

CATALOGUE OF WORKS

(Opus numbers after Op. 72, which are not Mendelssohn's own but were given to works posthumously published and are often chronologically misleading, are shown in brackets.)

OPERAS

Opus

10. *Die Hochzeit des Camacho*,[1] comic opera in 2 acts (1825).
(89.) *Die Heimkehr aus der Fremde*,[2] operetta in 1 act (1829).
(98.) *Loreley*, unfinished opera [3] (1847).
    Also 5 operas in manuscript.

INCIDENTAL MUSIC

55. *Antigone* (Sophocles) (1841).
61. *A Midsummer Night's Dream* [4] (Shakespeare) (1842).
(74.) *Athalie* (Racine) (1843–5).
(93.) *Oedipus at Colonus* (Sophocles) (1845).
(94.) *See* Orchestral Works and Voice and Orchestra for music for
    Victor Hugo's *Ruy Blas*.

---

[1] Properly Gamacho, as in Cervantes's *Don Quixote*, on an episode from which this work is based.

[2] Known as *Son and Stranger* in England.

[3] Finale of Act I, 'Ave Maria' for soprano and women's chorus, and Vintage Song for men's chorus only.

[4] For the overture, Op. 21, composed in 1826, *see* Orchestral Works. Also music for Calderón's *The Steadfast Prince* in manuscript.

Church Music

Opus

23.   3 Sacred Pieces for solo voice, chorus and organ (1830).
    1. *Aus tiefer Not.*
    2. *Ave Maria.*
    3. *Mitten wir im Leben sind.*

31.   Psalm CXV, *Non nobis, Domine,* for solo voices, chorus and orchestra (1830).

39.   3 Motets for women's chorus and organ (1830).
    1. *Veni, Domine.*
    2. *Laudate pueri.*
    3. *Surrexit Pastor.*

    Verleih' uns Frieden, prayer for chorus and orchestra (1831).
    Lord, have mercy upon us, anthem for the Anglican service for unaccompanied chorus (1833).

42.   Psalm XLII, *As pants the hart,* for solo voices, chorus and orchestra (1837).
    Defend me, Lord, from shame, hymn-tune for unaccompanied chorus (1839).

46.   Psalm XCV, *Come, let us sing,* for solo voices, chorus and orchestra (1839).

51.   Psalm CXIV, *When Israel out of Egypt came,* for eight-part chorus and orchestra (1839).

69.   3 English Church Pieces for solo voices and chorus (1847).
    1. *Nunc dimittis.*
    2. *Jubilate.*
    3. *Magnificat.*

(78.)   3 Psalms (1843–4).
    1. II, *Why rage fiercely the heathen?* for double chorus.
    2. XXII, *My God, My God,* for double chorus.
    3. XLIII, *Judge me, O God,* for eight-part chorus.
    Hymn, *Hear my prayer,* for soprano, chorus and organ (1844).

(79.)   6 Anthems (1843–6).
    1. *Rejoice, O ye people.*
    2. *Thou, Lord, our refuge hast been.*
    3. *Above all praises.*
    4. *Lord, on our offences.*

Opus

    5. Let our hearts be joyful.

    6. For our offences.

(91.) Psalm XCVIII, *Sing to the Lord a new-made song,* for eight-part chorus and orchestra (1843).

(96.) Hymn for contralto, chorus and orchestra (1840–3).[1]

(111.) *Tu es Petrus,* for five-part chorus and orchestra (1827).

    Kyrie eleison (Deutsche Liturgie), for five-part chorus (1846).

    Te Deum and *Jubilate* for the Anglican service, for chorus and organ (1846).

(115.) 2 Sacred Choruses for men's voices.

    1. *Beati mortui.*

    2. *Periti autem.*

(121.) *Responsorium et Hymnus,* for men's chorus, cello and organ.

    Magnificat and *Nunc dimittis* for the Anglican service, for chorus and organ.

    3 Sacred Choruses.

        1. *Ehre sei Gott,* double chorus.

        2. *Heilig,* double chorus.

        3. Psalm C.

        Also motets in manuscript.

ACCOMPANIED CHORAL WORKS

(with orchestra unless otherwise mentioned)

36. Oratorio, *St. Paul* (1836).

50. No. 2. *Des Jägers Abschied* (Eichendorff), for men's voices with 4 horns and bass trombone (1840).

52. *Lobgesang (Hymn of Praise),* symphony-cantata (Symphony No. 2) (1840).

    Festgesang for the Gutenberg Festival,[2] for men's chorus and orchestra (1840).

---

[1] Extension of 3 sacred songs for contralto, chorus and organ, published without opus number.

[2] No. 2 adapted as the Christmas hymn *Hark! the herald-angels sing.*

Opus

60. *Die erste Walpurgisnacht* (Goethe) (1st version 1832, 2nd 1843).
68. *An die Künstler: Festgesang* (Schiller), for men's voices and brass (1846).
70. Oratorio *Elijah* (1846).
(73.) Cantata *Lauda Sion* (1846).
(97.) Oratorio *Christus* (unfinished, recitative and choruses only). Also 3 sacred cantatas and one secular cantata.

UNACCOMPANIED CHORAL WORKS

41. 6 Partsongs for mixed voices (1834).
    1. *Im Walde* (Platen).
    2. *Entflieh' mit mir.*
    3. *Es fiel ein Reif.* } *Drei Volkslieder* (Heine).
    4. *Auf ihrem Grab.*
    5. *Mailied* (Hölty).
    6. *Auf dem See* (Goethe).
48. *Der erste Frühlingstag,* 6 partsongs for mixed voices (1839).
    1. *Frühlingsahnung* (Uhland).
    2. *Die Primel* (Lenau).
    3. *Frühlingsfeier* (Uhland).
    4. *Lerchengesang* (canon) (?).
    5. *Morgengebet* (Eichendorff).
    6. *Herbstlied* (Lenau).

    Ersatz für Unbestand (Rückert), for men's voices (1839).
50. 6 Partsongs for men's voices (1839–40).
    1. *Türkisches Schenkenlied* (Goethe).
    2. *See* Accompanied Choral Works.
    3. *Sommerlied* (Goethe).
    4. *Wasserfahrt* (Heine).
    5. *Liebe und Wein* (?).
    6. *Wanderlied* (Eichendorff).

    Nachtgesang (?), for men's voices (1842).
    Die Stiftungsfeier (?), for men's voices (1842).

Appendix B—Catalogue of Works

Mendelssohn

ORCHESTRAL WORKS

Opus

11. Symphony No. 1,[1] C minor (1824).
21. Overture to Shakespeare's *A Midsummer Night's Dream* (1826).
24. *Ouvertüre für Harmoniemusik* (1824).
26. Concert overture *Die Hebriden* (or *Die Fingalshöhle*) (1st version, *Die einsame Insel*, 1830; 2nd, 1832).
27. Concert overture *Meersstille und glückliche Fahrt*, on Goethe's twin poems (1828–32).
32. Concert overture *Das Märchen von der schönen Melusine*, on Grillparzer's opera libretto (1833).
52. *See* Accompanied Choral Works for Symphony No. 2.
56. Symphony No. 3, A minor-major ('Scottish') (1830–42).
(90.) Symphony No. 4, A major-minor ('Italian') (1833).
(95.) Overture to Victor Hugo's *Ruy Blas* (1839).
(101.) Overture in C major ('Trumpet' Overture) (1829).
(103.) *Trauermarsch*, in memory of Norberg Burgmüller, for military band (1836).
(107.) Symphony No. 5, D major ('Reformation') (1830–2).
(108.) March in D major (1841).
Symphony for strings in D major (1822) (later rewritten for full orchestra).
Symphony for strings in C major (1823).
Also 9 symphonies and numerous fugues for strings, a symphony for full orchestra and an overture in manuscript.

SOLO INSTRUMENTS AND ORCHESTRA

22. *Capriccio brillant*, B minor, for piano (1832).
25. Piano Concerto No. 1, G minor (1831).
29. *Rondo brillant*, E flat major, for piano (1834).
40. Piano Concerto No. 2, D minor (1837).
43. *Serenade* and *Allegro gioioso*, B minor, for piano (1838).

---

[1] Actually the thirteenth symphony, if the twelve remaining in manuscript are counted.

Appendix B—Catalogue of Works

64. Violin Concerto, E minor-major (1844).
    Also concertos (1 for piano, 1 for violin, 1 for violin and piano
        with strings and 2 for 2 pianos and orchestra) in manuscript.
    Violin Concerto in D minor (1822).
    Concerto for two pianos in E major (1823).
    Concerto for two pianos in A flat major (1824).

VOICE AND ORCHESTRA

(94.) Concert aria, *Infelice*, for soprano (1st version, 1834; 2nd, 1843).
    Song for Victor Hugo's *Ruy Blas* for soprano and strings (1839).

CHAMBER MUSIC

1. Piano Quartet No. 1, C minor (1822).
   String Quartet, E flat major (1823).[1]
2. Piano Quartet No. 2, F minor (1823).
3. Piano Quartet No. 3, B minor (1824-5).
12. String Quartet No. 1, E flat major (1829).
13. String Quarter No. 2, A major (1827).
18. String Quintet No. 1, A major (1st version, 1826; 2nd, 1832).
20. String Octet, E flat major (1825).
44. 3 String Quartets (1837-8).
    No. 3, D major.   No. 4, E minor.   No. 5, E flat major.
49. Piano Trio No. 1, D minor (1839).
66. Piano Trio No. 2, C minor (1845).
(80.) String Quartet No. 6, F minor (1847).
(81.) 4 pieces for string quartet.
    1. Andante, E major (1847).
    2. Scherzo, A minor (1847).
    3. Capriccio, E minor (1843).
    4. Fugue, E flat major (1827).
(87.) String Quintet No. 2, B flat major (1845).
(110.) Sextet for violin, 2 violas, cello, double bass and piano, D major
    (1824).

---

[1] Not numbered by the composer and thus probably not intended
by him for publication.

Opus

(113.) *Concertstück* No. 1, F minor, for clarinet, basset horn and piano (1833).

(114.) *Concertstück* No. 2, D minor, for clarinet, basset horn and piano (1833).

Also a Trio for violin, cello and piano in manuscript.

VIOLIN AND PIANO

4. Sonata, F minor (1825).

Also 2 sonatas in manuscript (one dated 1838).

Sonata, F major (1938).

VIOLONCELLO AND PIANO

17. *Variations concertantes*, D major (1829).
45. Sonata No. 1, B flat major (1838).
58. Sonata No. 2, D major (1843).
(109.) *Song without Words*, D major (1845).

Also a Sonata for viola and piano and a Sonata for clarinet and piano in manuscript.

HARP AND PIANO

The Evening Bell (1829).[1]

CLARINET AND PIANO

Sonata in E flat major (1825).

PIANO SOLO

5. *Capriccio*, F sharp minor (1825).
6. Sonata, E major (1826).
7. 7 Characteristic Pieces (various dates, published 1927).
    1. *Sanft und mit Empfindung*, E minor.
    2. *Mit heftiger Bewegung*, B minor.
    3. *Kräftig und feurig*, D major.
    4. *Schnell und beweglich*, A major.
    5. *Fuga: ernst und mit steigender Lebhaftigkeit*, A major.
    6. *Sehnsüchtig*, E minor.
    7. *Leicht und luftig*, E major.

---

[1] Suggested by the bell at the gate of Attwood's house at Norwood.

Appendix B—Catalogue of Works

Opus

   3. *Presto,* E major.

   4. *Andante,* A major.

   5. *Agitato,* A minor.

   6. *Andante con moto,* A flat major (Duetto).

   Andante cantabile and *Presto agitato,* B major (1838).

53. Songs without Words, Book IV (1841).

   1. *Andante con moto,* A flat major.

   2. *Allegro non troppo,* E flat major.

   3. *Presto agitato,* G minor.

   4. *Adagio,* F major.

   5. *Allegro,* A minor (*Volkslied*).

   6. *Molto allegro vivace,* A major.

54. *Variations sérieuses,* D minor (1841).

   Prelude and Fugue, E minor (1827 [Fugue]–1841 [Prelude]).

62. Songs without Words, Book V (1842–4).

   1. *Andante espressivo,* G major.

   2. *Allegro con fuoco,* B major.

   3. *Andante maestoso,* E minor (*Trauermarsch*).

   4. *Allegro con anima,* G major.

   5. *Andante,* A minor (*Venetian Gondola Song*).

   6. *Allegretto grazioso,* A major (*Frühlingslied*).

67. Songs without Words, Book VI (1843–5).

   1. *Andante,* E flat major.

   2. *Allegro leggiero,* F sharp minor.

   3. *Andante tranquillo,* B flat major.

   4. *Presto,* C major (*Spinnerlied: The Bee's Wedding*).

   5. *Moderato,* B minor.

   6. *Allegro non troppo,* E major.

72. *Kinderstücke* (*Christmas Pieces*) (1842).

   1. *Allegro non troppo,* G major.

   2. *Andante sostenuto,* E flat major.

   3. *Allegretto,* G major.

   4. *Andante con moto,* D major.

   5. *Allegro assai,* G minor.

   6. *Vivace,* F major.

(82.) Variations, E flat major (1841).

(83.) Variations, B flat major (1841).

Appendix B—Catalogue of Works

Opus

(85.) Songs without Words, Book VII (1834–47).
1. *Andante espressivo,* F major.
2. *Allegro agitato,* A minor.
3. *Presto,* E flat major.
4. *Andante sostenuto,* D major.
5. *Allegretto,* A major.
6. *Allegretto con moto,* B flat major.

(102.) Songs without Words, Book VIII (1842–5).
1. *Andante un poco agitato,* E minor.
2. *Adagio,* D major.
3. *Presto,* C major.
4. *Un poco agitato,* G minor.
5. *Allegro vivace,* A major (*Kinderstück*).
6. *Andante,* C major.

(104.) Book I: 3 Preludes (1836).
1. B flat major.
2. B minor.
3. D major.

Book II: 3 Studies.
1. B flat minor (1836).
2. F major (1834).
3. A minor (1838).

(105.) Sonata, G minor (1821).
(106.) Sonata, B flat major (1827).
(117.) *Albumblatt,* E minor (1837).
(118.) *Capriccio,* E major.
(119.) *Perpetuum mobile,* C major.
Scherzo, B minor.
Scherzo a capriccio, F minor.
Zwei Clavierstücke.
1. *Andante cantabile,* B flat major.
2. *Presto agitato,* G minor.
Also 2 sonatas and numerous studies, fantasies, fugues, etc., in manuscript.

PIANOFORTE DUETS

Opus
(83*a*.) Variations, B flat major (arr. from Op. 83 for piano solo).
 (92.) *Allegro brillant*, A major (1841).
    Duo concertant, Variations on the March from Weber's *Preciosa* (with Moscheles) [1] (1833).
       Also a Fantasy in manuscript.

ORGAN MUSIC

37. 3 Preludes and Fugues (1833–9).
    1. C minor.
    2. G major.
    3. D minor.
  Fugue, F minor (1839).
  Prelude, C minor (1841).
  2 Pieces (1844).
    1. *Andante and Variations*, D major.
    2. *Allegro*, B flat major.
65. 6 Sonatas (1839–45).
    1. F minor-major.
    2. C minor-major.
    3. A major.
    4. B flat major.
    5. D major.
    6. D minor-major.
      Also numerous fugues in manuscript.

SONGS

8. 12 Songs (published 1830).
    1. *Minnelied* (Hölty)

---

[1] Originally for 2 pianos and orchestra.

Opus

    (2. *Das Heimweh* (Friederike Robert).) [1]
    (3. *Italien* (Grillparzer).)
    4. *Erntelied* (traditional).
    5. *Pilgerspruch* (Paul Flemming).
    6. *Frühlingslied* (F. Robert).
    7. *Maienlied* (Jakob von der Warte).
    8. *Hexenlied* (Hölty).
    9. *Abendlied* (J. H. Voss).
    10. *Romanze* (from the Spanish).
    11. *Im Grünen* (Voss).
    (12. *Suleika und Hatem* (Goethe), duet.)

9. 12 Songs (1829).
    1. *Frage* (Voss).
    2. *Geständnis* (?).
    3. *Wartend* (*Romanze*) (?).
    4. *Im Frühling* (?).
    5. *Im Herbst* (Karl Klingemann).
    6. *Scheidend* (Voss)
    (7. *Sehnsucht* (J. G. Droysen).)
    8. *Frühlingsglaube* (Uhland).
    9. *Ferne* (Droysen).
    (10. *Verlust* (Heine).)
    11. *Entsagung* (Droysen).
    (12. *Die Nonne* (Uhland).)

The Garland (Thomas Moore) (1829).
Seemanns Scheidelied (Hoffmann von Fallersleben) (1831).

19a. 6 Songs.
    1. *Frühlingslied* (Ulrich von Lichtenstein).
    2. *Das erste Veilchen* (Egon Ebert).
    3. *Winterlied* (from the Swedish).
    4. *Neue Liebe* (Heine).
    5. *Gruss* (Heine).
    6. *Reiselied* (Ebert) (1830).

---

[1] Op. 8, Nos. 2, 3, 12, and Op. 9, Nos. 7, 10, 12 are by Fanny Mendelssohn.

Mendelssohn

Opus
(84.) 3 Songs (1831–9).
    1. *Da lieg' ich unter den Bäumen* (?).
    2. *Herbstlied* (Klingemann).
    3. *Jagdlied* (from *Des Knaben Wunderhorn*).
(86.) 6 Songs (1826–47).
    1. *Es lausche das Laub* (Klingemann).
    2. *Morgenlied* (?).
    3. *Die Liebende schreibt* (Goethe).
    4. *Allnächtlich im Traume* (Heine).
    5. *Der Mond* (Geibel).
    6. *Altdeutsches Frühlingslied* (Spee).
(99.) 6 Songs (1841–5).
    1. *Erster Verlust* (Goethe).
    2. *Die Sterne schau'n* (A. von Schlippenbach).
    3. *Lieblingsplätzchen* (from *Des Knaben Wunderhorn*).
    4. *Das Schifflein* (Uhland).
    5. *Wenn sich zwei Herzen scheiden* (Geibel).
    6. *Es weiss und rät es doch Keiner* (Eichendorff).
(112.) 2 Sacred Songs (1835).
    1. *Doch der Herr, er leitet den Irrenden recht.*
    2. *Der du die Menschen lässest sterben.*[1]
    Des Mädchens Klage (Schiller).
    Warnung vor dem Rhein (C. Simrock).
    Also songs in manuscript.

VOCAL DUETS WITH PIANO

63. 6 Duets (1836–44).
    1. *Ich wollt' meine Lieb' ergösse* (Heine).
    2. *Abschiedslied der Zugvögel* (Hoffmann von Fallersleben).
    3. *Gruss* (Eichendorff).
    4. *Herbstlied* (Klingemann).
    5. *Volkslied* (Burns).
    6. *Maiglöckchen und die Blümelein* (Hoffmann von Fallersleben).

---

[1] Originally intended for *St. Paul*.

Mendelssohn

Opus

(77.) 3 Duets (1836–47).

    1. *Sonntagsmorgen* (Uhland).

    2. *Das Aehrenfeld* (Hoffmann von Fallersleben).

    3. *Lied aus 'Ruy Blas'* (Victor Hugo).

Drei Volkslieder.

    1. *Wie kann ich froh und lustig sein?* (P. Kaufmann).

    2. *Abendlied* (Heine).

    3. *Wasserfahrt* (Heine).

EDITIONS AND ARRANGEMENTS

Bach's *Chaconne* arranged with piano accompaniment.

Preludes and other organ works by Bach edited.

Bach's Variations on the chorale *Sei gegrüsset, Jesu gütig,* edited from the original manuscript.

Additional accompaniments for Handel's *Acis and Galatea.*

Additional accompaniments for Handel's Dettingen *Te Deum.*

Organ part for Handel's *Israel in Egypt.*

Organ part for Handel's *Solomon.*

APPENDIX C

Adams, Thomas (1785–1858), organist in London and composer for his instrument.

Anderson, Lucy, née Philpot (1797–1878), pianist in London, teacher of Queen Victoria.

André, Julius (1808–80), son of the founder of the publishing firm of André, Offenbach-on-Main. Pianist, organist and composer.

Attwood, Thomas (1765–1838), organist and composer in London. Pupil of Mozart in Vienna. Organist of St. Paul's Cathedral, 1796–1838.

Ayrton, William (1777–1858), writer on music in London. Editor of the *Harmonicon*; musical contributor to the *Morning Chronicle* and the *Examiner*.

Bache, Walter (1842–88), pianist in London; pupil and disciple of Liszt.

Baillot, Pierre Marie François de Sales (1771–1842), French violinist.

Baini, Abbate Giuseppe (1775–1844), singer in the Pontifical Chapel, Rome; composer of a *Miserere*, produced in Rome, 1821.

Bärmann, Heinrich Joseph (1784–1847), clarinet player, for whom Weber wrote three concertos and Mendelssohn the duos for clarinet and basset-horn.

Bartholomew, William (1793–1867), scientific chemist, violinist and hymn writer. Author of the English texts of Mendelssohn's chief choral works.

Becker, Carl Ferdinand (1804–77), organist in Leipzig.

Benedict, Julius (1804–85), German composer and pianist settled in England.

Bennett, William Sterndale (1816–75), composer and pianist. Professor of Music, Cambridge University, 1856–75.

Berger, Ludwig (1777–1839), pianist in Berlin.

Bériot, Charles de (1802–70), Belgian violinist and composer.

Bigot, Marie, née Kiene (1786–1820), Alsatian pianist in Paris and Vienna.
Birch, Charlotte Anne (1815–1901), English soprano singer.
Braham, John (1777–1856), English tenor singer and composer.
Bull, Ole Borneman (1810–80), Norwegian violinist.

Caradori-Allan, Maria Caterina Rosalbina, née de Munck (1800–65), English soprano singer.
Chorley, Henry Fothergill (1808–72), journalist, novelist and music critic in London.
Cramer, François (1772–1848), German violinist settled in London. Brother of J. B. Cramer. For many years leader of the Philharmonic orchestra.
Cramer, Johann Baptist (1771–1858), German pianist and composer settled in London. Occasional conductor of the Philharmonic concerts, 1813–34.

David, Ferdinand (1810–73), German violinist and composer.
Davison, James William (1813–85), music critic in London.
Devrient, Eduard Philipp (1801–77), German baritone singer and actor.
Dolby, Charlotte Helen (1821–85), English contralto singer and composer.
Dorn, Heinrich Ludwig Egmont (1804–92), conductor and composer. Conductor, Royal Opera, Berlin, 1847–68.
Dussek, Jan Ladislav (1760–1812), Czech composer and pianist.

Fétis, François Joseph (1784–1871), Belgian musical historian, essayist and composer. Author of the *Biographie Universelle des Musiciens*.
Fodor-Mainvielle, Joséphine (1789–1870), French soprano singer.
Franchomme, Auguste (1808–84), French violoncellist.
Frege, Livia, née Gerhard (1818–91), German singer living in Leipzig after her marriage in 1836.

Gade, Niels Vilhelm (1817–90), Danish composer.
Gauntlett, Henry John (1805–76), English organist and composer, Mus.Doc.
Goldschmidt, Otto (1829–1907), German pianist and composer, accompanist and afterwards husband of Jenny Lind (q.v.). Founder of the Bach Choir, London.
Grisi, Giulia (1811–69), Italian operatic soprano.

Appendix C—Personalia

Grove, George (1820–1900), English civil engineer, Biblical scholar and writer on music. Secretary to the Crystal Palace Company, 1852–73; director, Royal College of Music, 1883–94. Editor of the *Dictionary of Music and Musicians*.

Habeneck, François Antoine (1781–1849), French violinist and conductor. Founder of the Société des Concerts du Conservatoire, Paris. Conductor at the Opera, 1824–47.

Hallé, Charles (1819–95), German pianist and conductor, settled in England from 1848; founder of the Hallé concerts in Manchester.

Hauptmann, Moritz (1792–1868), German theoretical writer and composer. Cantor of the St. Thomas School, Leipzig, from 1842 to his death.

Henselt, Adolph (1814–89), German pianist and composer.

Herz, Henri (1806–88), Austrian pianist, composer and piano maker settled in Paris.

Hiller, Ferdinand (1811–85), German composer, pianist and writer.

Hummel, Johann Nepomuk (1778–1837), pianist and composer.

Joachim, Joseph (1831–1907), Hungarian violinist and composer settled in Germany, but spending much time in England.

Kalkbrenner, Friedrich Wilhelm Michael (1788–1849), German pianist and composer settled in Paris.

Klingemann, Karl (1798–1862), secretary to the Hanoverian Legation in Berlin, and in London from 1828. Cultivated amateur and lyrical poet.

Knyvett, Deborah, née Travis (1796?–1876), English soprano singer. Married (as his second wife) to William Knyvett, alto vocalist and composer.

Lind, Jenny (1820–87), Swedish soprano singer settled in England; wife of Otto Goldschmidt (q.v.).

Lockey, Charles (1820–1901), English tenor singer. Married, 1853, the singer Martha Williams (1821–97).

Macfarren, George Alexander (1813–87), composer and theorist in London. Principal of the Royal Academy of Music, 1875–87. Professor of Music, Cambridge University.

Machin, William (1798–1870), English bass singer.

Malibran, Maria Felicità, née Garcia (1808–36), Franco-Spanish soprano singer, later the wife of Bériot (q.v.).

Mario, Giovanni, Conte de Candia (1810–83), Italian operatic tenor.

Marx, Adolph Bernhard (1795–1866), German composer, theorist and writer.

Milder-Hauptmann, Pauline Anna (1785–1838), German soprano singer.

Montfort, Alexandre (1804–56), French composer.

Moscheles, Ignaz (1794–1870), German pianist and composer, long settled in London.

Naumann, Emil (1827–88), German writer on music and composer.

Neukomm, Sigismund (1778–1858), Austrian amateur composer.

Novello, Clara Anastasia (1818–1908), soprano singer in London. Married Count Gigliucci in 1843.

Novello, Vincent (1781–1861), father of the preceding. Composer, organist and publisher in London.

Onslow, George (1784–1853), Anglo-French composer, living at Clermont-Ferrand and Paris.

Pasta, Giuditta, née Negri (1798–1865), Italian operatic soprano singer.

Phillips, Henry (1801–76), bass singer in London.

Piatti, Alfredo (1822–1901), Italian violoncellist living chiefly in London.

Pierson, Heinrich Hugo (real name Henry Hugh Pearson) (1815–73), English composer settled in Germany.

Pixis, Johann Peter (1788–1874), German pianist and composer settled in Paris.

Planché, James Robinson (1796–1880), English dramatist and librettist.

Pleyel, Camille (1788–1855), French pianist and piano manufacturer.

Pohlenz, Christian August (1790–1843), German organist and conductor. Organist, St. Thomas's, Leipzig, cantor, 1828; conductor, Gewandhaus concerts, 1827–35.

Rellstab, Heinrich Friedrich Ludwig (1799–1860), critic in Berlin.

Rietz, Eduard (1802–32), violinist in Berlin.

Rietz, Julius (1812–77), German composer and conductor, brother of the preceding.

Rinck, Johann Christian Heinrich (1770–1846), German organist, composer and teacher.

Appendix C—Personalia

Rockstro, William Smith (1823–95), organist, composer and writer in London.

Rungenhagen, Carl Friedrich (1778–1851), composer and conductor in Berlin.

Schelble, Johann Nepomuk (1789–1837), German conductor.

Schmitt, Aloys (1788–1866), German pianist and teacher.

Schneider, Friedrich Johann Christian (1786–1853), German composer and organist.

Schumann, Clara Josephine, née Wieck (1819–96), German pianist and composer. Wife of Robert Schumann.

Schunke, Carl (1801–39), German pianist.

Seidler, Caroline, née Wranitzki (1794–1872), Austrian soprano singer.

Shaw, Mary, née Postans (1814–76), English contralto singer.

Sivori, Ernesto Camillo (1815–94), Italian violinist, pupil of Paganini.

Smart, George Thomas (1776–1867), composer and conductor in London.

Spitta, August Philipp (1841–94), German musical historian and editor.

Staudigl, Joseph (1807–61), Austrian bass singer.

Stimpson, James (1820–86), organist in Birmingham.

Stümer, Johann Daniel Heinrich (1789–1857), German tenor singer.

Taubert, Karl Gottfried Wilhelm (1811–91), composer and conductor in Berlin.

Thalberg, Sigismond (1812–71), German pianist and composer.

Thibaut, Anton Friedrich Justus (1774–1840), writer on music. Professor of Law, Heidelberg University.

Unger, Caroline (1803–77), Austro-Hungarian contralto singer.

Verhulst, Johannes Josephus Herman (1816–91), Dutch composer and conductor at The Hague.

Viardot-Garcia, Michelle Pauline (1821–1910), Franco-Spanish soprano singer.

Wesley, Samuel (1766–1837), English organist and composer.

Wölfl, Joseph (1772–1812), Austrian pianist and composer.

Zelter, Carl Friedrich (1758–1832), composer, conductor and teacher in Berlin. Director of the Singakademie.

APPENDIX D

BIBLIOGRAPHY

Armstrong, Thomas, 'Mendelssohn's "Elijah."' ('Musical Pilgrim' series, Oxford, 1931.)

Barbedette, H., 'Felix Mendelssohn-Bartholdy: sa vie et ses œuvres.' (Paris, 1869.)

Bartels, Bernhard, 'Mendelssohn-Bartholdy: Mensch und Werk.' (Bremen and Hanover, 1947.)

Benedict, Julius, 'A Sketch of the Life and Works of the late Felix Mendelssohn-Bartholdy.' (London, 1850; second edition, 1853.)

Blunt, Wilfrid, 'On Wings of Song.' (Hamish Hamilton, 1974.)

Dahms, Walter, 'Mendelssohn.' (Berlin and Leipzig, 1919.)

Devrient, Eduard, 'Meine Erinnerungen an Felix Mendelssohn-Bartholdy.' (Leipzig, 1869.) English translation by Lady Macfarren. (London, 1869.)

Eckardt, Julius, 'Ferdinand David und die Familie Mendelssohn-Bartholdy.' (Leipzig, 1888.)

Edwards, F. G., 'The History of Mendelssohn's "Elijah."' (London, 1896.)

—— 'Mendelssohn's Organ Sonatas.' (Proc. Mus. Ass., Vol. XXI, 1894.)

Foss, Hubert, 'Felix Mendelssohn-Bartholdy,' in 'The Heritage of Music,' Vol. II. (Oxford, 1934.)

Gotch, Rosamund Brunel, 'Mendelssohn and his Friends in Kensington.' (Oxford, 1934.)

Grove, Sir George, 'Beethoven: Schubert: Mendelssohn.' (London, 1951.) Reprints of articles in Grove's Dictionary, first to fourth editions.

Hathaway, Joseph W. G., 'Analysis of Mendelssohn's Organ Works.' (London, n.d.)

Hensel, Sebastian, 'Die Familie Mendelssohn.' 3 vols. (Berlin, 1879.) English translation, 2 vols. (London, 1881.)

Hiller, Ferdinand, 'Mendelssohn: Letters and Recollections . . .' (Cologne, 1874). English translation by M. E. von Glehn. (London, 1874.)

Horsley, Charles Edward, 'Reminiscences of Mendelssohn' in *Dwight's Journal of Music* (Boston, Mass., 1872) and *The Choir* (London, 1873).

Horton, John, 'The Chamber Music of Mendelssohn.' ('Musical Pilgrim' series, Oxford, 1946.)

Jacob, H. E., 'Felix Mendelssohn and his Times.' (London, 1963.)

Jacob, Robert, 'Mendelssohn: a Revaluation.' (*Penguin Music Magazine,* Nos. 3 and 4, 1947.)

Kahl, Willi, 'Zu Mendelssohns Liedern ohne Worte.' (*Zeitschrift für Musikwissenshaft,* May 1921.)

Kaufmann, S., 'Mendelssohn, "a Second Elijah."' (New York, 1934.)

Lampadius, Wilhelm Adolf, 'Felix Mendelssohn-Bartholdy: ein Denkmal für seine Freunde.' (Leipzig, 1849.) English translation by W. L. Gage, with supplementary sketches by various authors. (New York, 1866; London, 1876.)

Magnien, Victor, 'Étude biographique sur Mendelssohn-Bartholdy.' (Beauvais, 1850.)

Mariotti, Giovanni, 'Mendelssohn.' (Rome, 1937.)

Mendelssohn-Bartholdy, Carl, 'Goethe und Felix Mendelssohn-Bartholdy.' (Leipzig, 1871.)

Mendelssohn-Bartholdy, Felix, 'Acht Briefe und ein Facsimile.' (Leipzig, 1871.) English translation in *Macmillan's Magazine,* June 1871.

—— 'Briefe aus den Jahren 1833 bis 1847,' edited by Paul Mendelssohn. (Leipzig, 1863.) English translation by Lady Wallace. (London, 1863.)

—— 'Briefe . . . an Ignaz und Charlotte Moscheles,' edited by Felix Moscheles. (Leipzig, 1888.) English translation. (London, 1888.)

—— Letters (30) dating from 1826 to 1847 in Ludwig Nohl's 'Musikerbriefe.' (Leipzig, 1867.) English translation, 'Letters of Distinguished Musicians,' by Lady Wallace. (London, 1867.)

—— Letters, edited by Gisela Selden-Goth. (New York, 1945.)

Mendelssohn

Mendelssohn-Bartholdy, Felix, 'Reisebriefe . . . aus den Jahren 1830 bis 1832,' edited by Paul Mendelssohn. (Leipzig, 1861.) English translation by Lady Wallace. (London, 1862.)

Meyerstein, E. H. W., 'Some Remarks on the Genius of Mendelssohn.' (*Music Survey*, No. 2, 1948.)

Neumann, W., 'F. Mendelssohn-Bartholdy: eine Biographie.' (Cassel, 1854.)

Petitpierre, Jacques, 'The Romance of the Mendelssohns.' (London, 1948.)

Polko, Elise, 'Erinnerungen an Felix Mendelssohn-Bartholdy.' (Leipzig, 1868.) English translation by Lady Wallace. (London, 1869.)

Reissmann, August, 'Felix Mendelssohn-Bartholdy: sein Leben und seine Werke.' (Berlin, 1867.)

Rockstro, W. S., 'Mendelssohn.' (London, 1884.)

Selden, Camille, 'La Musique en Allemagne. Mendelssohn.' (Paris, 1867.)

Schubring, Julius, 'Erinnerungen an Felix Mendelssohn-Bartholdy' in *Daheim*. (Leipzig, 1866.) English translation in *The Musical World*. (London, 1866.)

Schünemann, Georg, 'Mendelssohn's Jugendopern.' (*Zeitschrift für Musikwissenschaft*, June–July 1923.)

Sterndale Bennett, R., 'The Death of Mendelssohn.' (*Music & Letters*, XLVI, 1965.)

Tischler, Louise H. and Hans, 'Mendelssohn's Style.' (*Music Review*, VIII, 1947, p. 256.)

Walker, Ernest, 'Concerning an Oxford Collection of Mendelssohniana.' (*Music & Letters*, XIX, 1938.)

Werner, Eric, 'Mendelssohn.' Translated by Dika Newlin. (New York, 1963.)

Werner, Jack, 'Felix and Fanny Mendelssohn.' (*Music & Letters*, XXVIII, 1947.)

—— 'Mendelssohn's "Elijah."' (London, 1965.)

Werner, Rudolf, 'Felix Mendelssohn-Bartholdy als Kirchenmusiker.' (Frankfort o/M., 1930.)

Winn, Cyril, 'Mendelssohn.' ('Musical Pilgrim' series, Oxford, 1928.)

INDEX

Index

Index

Index

Index

Index

Index